TRANSRACIAL ADOPTEES
AND
THEIR FAMILIES

TRANSRACIAL ADOPTEES
AND
THEIR FAMILIES

A Study of Identity
and
Commitment

Rita J. Simon
and
Howard Altstein

PRAEGER

New York
Westport, Connecticut
London

Library of Congress Cataloging-in-Publication Data

Simon, Rita James.
  Transracial adoptees and their families.

  Bibliography: p.
  Includes index.
  1. Interracial adoption – United States –
Longitudinal studies.   2. Children, Adopted –
United States – Family relationships – Longitudinal
studies.   3. Race awareness in children –
United States – Longitudinal studies.   I. Altstein,
Howard.   II. Title.
HV875.64.S56   1987   362.7'34   86-30332
ISBN 0-275-92398-3 (alk. paper)

Library of Congress Catalog Card Number: 86-30332
ISBN: 0-275-92398-3

First published in 1987

Praeger Publishers, 521 Fifth Avenue, New York, NY 10175
A division of Greenwood Press, Inc.

Printed in the United States of America

The paper used in this book complies with the Permanent
Paper Standard issued by the National Information Standards
Organization (Z39.48-1984).

10 9 8 7 6 5 4 3 2 1

To
David, Judith, and Daniel
and to
Samuel and Rachel

Contents

Acknowledgments

We have two special debts of gratitude. The first is to the families who participated in the study starting in 1972. Their patience, interest, and candor are deeply appreciated. We hope we described their experiences with as much dignity and understanding as they lived them. The second is to the William T. Grant Foundation for providing us with the funds to conduct the study.

In addition, we acknowledge with appreciation and thanks the work of our field staff. Their commitment to the study and their tenacity in locating families and conducting interviews that sometimes lasted three or four hours went far beyond usual professional standards. Specifically, we want to thank our interviewers: Sharon Carter, William Fickling, Dottie Gilvin, Carol Hartman, Cheryl Johnson, Jackie Smith, Marcy Rasmussen, Brad Richardson, Yosikazu De Roos, Virginia Sykes, and Mauricia Treadwell. Professors Mildred Schwartz, Sarah Boggs, and Roberta Simmons helped us locate our field staff.

Finally, we want to express our thanks to Mike Schlesinger for her devotion, unending patience, and care in the typing of this manuscript, and to Gloria Danzinger for her help editing the final draft.

Rita J. Simon
The American University

Howard Altstein
University of Maryland

Introduction

The heart of this volume is Part II. It reports the results of the third phase of our study of transracial adoption, in which we interviewed 96 parents and 218 children, 111 of whom have been transracially adopted, 91 of whom have been born into the families, and 16 of whom have been adopted. This third phase occurred four and a half years after our last contacts with these families and twelve years after we interviewed them for the first time.

The data collected in this phase were aimed at answering questions about the long-term effects of transracial adoption on the adoptees and their siblings, about the adoptees' racial identities and self-esteem, and about the strength of the loyalties and commitments the parents and children have toward each other.

Personal interviews were conducted with both parents and each child, separately and privately. The parents were asked to go back in time and tell us about their successes and failures, and their pains and pleasures as a result of their decision to adopt a child of a different race. We asked that they look into the future and try to project the quality of the relationship they are likely to have with their transracially adopted child(ren), and the ties that the siblings are likely to have with each other when the children leave the family home. We also asked that they tell us about how they perceive each of their children's racial identities, scholastic and career achievements and aspirations, about their choice of friends and dates, and the decisions their children are likely to make about marriage partners and types of communities in which they will choose to live.

From the adolescents we sought information about their sense of belonging in the family, the siblings' ties to each other, how they described themselves racially and socially, their scholastic and career goals, and most of all, their feelings about having been transracially adopted.

All of the families studied had completed their first transracial adoption before 1972. They experienced disappointment and surprise at the attacks by the National Association of Black Social Workers and Native American Councils on the practice of placing black and native American children in white homes. They listened to the warnings about the likelihood that they would rear "Oreos" (children who would be black on the outside and white on the inside), who would not be able to cope with their special status.

In phases one and two, we reported that the parents were optimistic that their children would have integrated and wholesome personalities and the emotional security sufficient to allow them to make their way and gain acceptance among both black and white communities. Rather than becoming the pariahs that the Black Social Workers warned about, these children would also become part of a small but growing integrated community in which race was not a major basis for acceptance or evaluation. Phase three assesses the likelihood that the parents' hopes have and will be realized and that the transracial adoptees are aware of their "special status" and capable of coping with it.

We begin this volume by providing, in Part I, what statistical data are available on the numbers of transracial adoptions nationally, practices of adoption agencies, and recent court rulings. Part I also discusses the positions of the National Association of Black Social Workers, Child Welfare League, and other agencies, public and private, involved in the placement of nonwhite children.

Part III examines alternative forms of adoption such as single parent adoption. It reports the effects of contraceptive practices and abortions among teenagers on birth rates and adoptions; and it provides data and analysis about intercountry adoptions.

Part I

1

Where We Are Today: Numbers, Practices, and Policies

Adoption Supervisor: There will be many social problems when the child eventually leaves home, leaves the protected environment...what is life going to be like for him...at age 18?[1]

Adoptive Applicant: Does any social service agency have the right to deprive a child of a home?[2]

State's Attorney: Race is not a bar to adoption.[3]

Such were the statements made in July 1984 by a black county adoption supervisor, a white adoptive applicant, and a state's attorney about a white couple's attempt to adopt a mildly retarded black three-year-old suffering from a form of cerebral palsy and poor vision. The child had been in their foster care since birth.

. A belief that transracial adoption (TRA) is unnatural and therefore "bound to be unsuccessful" continues to be popular among many child welfare professionals. Many adoption officials claim that there are studies that indicate that TRA is too fragile an experience not to result in serious problems once the TRAs leave their families.[4] But to this date no data have been presented that support the belief that in the long run TRA is detrimental to those involved: the transracial adoptees, the adoptive parents, or the siblings. On the contrary, evidence accumulated by us and other researchers over more than a decade of investigating the effects of TRA indicates positive results.[5]

Discussing a recent study on children of (racial) intermarriage, Alvin Poussaint observed, "We have lots of reasons to suspect that an interracial background can be an advantage to children in this society...[and that they] may be a more successful group in this society than has previously been believed."[6] Although referring to children with racially different parents, the fact that these children live in both the black and white worlds makes them

3

in many important respects similar to the children described in our study. Moreover, since interracial marriage between whites and blacks is increasing, there is a strong likelihood that increasing numbers of interracial children will be born. For example, from 1970 to 1980 the number of interracial marriages in the United States approximately doubled, from 310,000 couples in 1970 to 613,000 in 1980. The latter represents about 1.3 percent of all marriages recorded in the United States.[7] While on a nationwide scale these numbers appear miniscule, such marriages will no doubt produce thousands of children who will have experiences similar to those of transracially adopted children.

INRACIAL ADOPTION

In 1975, the federal government stopped collecting data on the number of adoptions. Any discussion, therefore, of national adoption trends is quite simply a guessing game. No individual, group, or institution has any reliable national figures on the number of adoptions, inracial or transracial, occurring in the United States in the mid-1980s. We do have statistical projections, educated guesses, and, in varying degrees, informed opinions. An interesting development, and a testimonial, in our opinion, to the future of adoptions in the United States is that the federal government has extremely accurate figures on intercountry adoptions. These figures, collected by the Department of Justice, Immigration and Naturalization Service, indicate that in the 12-month period ending September 30, 1984, 7,848 children entered this country for adoption purposes.[8] The intercountry adoption phenomenon will be discussed in more detail in a later chapter.

In 1975, the last year of federal reporting, approximately 129,000 children were adopted, down from about 175,000 adoptions in 1970, but significantly higher than 1951, when an estimated 72,000 adoptions were reported.[9] The above figures are of limited accuracy insofar as not all 50 states reported and in some instances the data from reporting states are incomplete.

In March 1985, the National Center for Health Statistics (NCHS) estimated that approximately 67,700 biologically unrelated adoptions occurred in 1981.[10] This figure, however, has a standard error of 29,900, which means that the true number of such adoptions was somewhere between 7,900 and 127,500 (plus or minus two standard deviations). It is interesting to note that although most people assume adoption usually occurs between children and unrelated adults, historically, adoption by family members has accounted for the majority of the adoptions. For example, in 1975, unrelated adoptions constituted only 37 percent of the total number.[11]

In a March 1985 interview, the president of the National Committee for Adoption indicated that a low estimate of the number of inracial adoptions occurring that year was around 65,000. He cautioned, however, that in all likelihood there were "huge numbers of unreported adoptions."[12] In April 1985, *Science '85* reported that there were approximately 65,000 adoptions per year.[13] It was from the National Committee that *Science '85* received its 65,000 figure. But the Child Welfare Indicator Survey, 1982, reported that of the approximately 50,000 children available for adoption during that year, only 17,000 actually were adopted.[14]

TRANSRACIAL ADOPTION

If it is difficult to predict with any degree of accuracy the number of inracial adoptions occurring in the United States since 1975, it is virtually impossible to place even the most general figure on the number of transracial adoptions. As in the case of overall adoption figures, there are some informed guesses, statistical projections, and demographic deductions. But they are weaker and less convincing than general adoption figures and require a greater leap of faith. Most informed individuals, including the authors, believe that both public and private child welfare agencies arrange TRAs, but neither group will publicly admit to doing so. TRA continues to be identified in most areas as a highly charged racial issue and a rallying point symbolic of historic grievances. Most adoption agencies would rather not draw attention to themselves by actively supporting or encouraging this type of child placement.

What data, then, are available? Again, we turn to 1975. In that year the Department of Health, Education, and Welfare reported 831 TRAs, down from its recorded high of 2,574 in 1971.[15] In April 1983, the North American Council on Adoptable Children (NACAC) reported that federal authorities (presumably the Department of Health and Human Services [DHHS]) estimated the number of children in foster care to be "approximately 500,000–750,000," 60 percent of whom were racial or ethnic minorities.[16] Approximately 100,000–120,000 children in foster care were legally free for adoption; about 30 percent of these were black.[17] Thus, relying only on the rough figures suggested by the foster care system, we estimate that there should be about 33,000–40,000 black children awaiting adoption placement.

But one year later, in 1984, DHHS reported that in 1982 there were only 243,000 children in foster care, of whom 50,000 were free for adoption.[18]

Number of Children in Foster Care
and Free for Adoption (in parentheses)

1977	1982
500,000	243,000
(102,000)	(50,000)

Also in 1984, the president of the National Committee for Adoption suggested that of the approximately 2 million white couples who would like to adopt, about 68,000 would do so transracially. If that were in fact to happen, all the black children available for adoption would have homes with white parents.

In short, the disparity among the figures, some of which came from the same federal agency, highlights the difficulties in establishing a credible count of adoptions since 1975. Indeed, the level of our knowledge regarding available adoptable children can be summed up by quoting a statistician employed at the Administration for Children, Youth, and Families: "There are no reliable national statistics available on virtually all...aspects of adoption."[19]

AGENCY PRACTICES

The quote from the supervisor that appeared at the beginning of this chapter is worthy of further examination because it encapsulates the stubborn myths about transracial adoption. These unfounded ideas have been largely if not totally responsible for the almost complete demise of this type of adoption.

A childless white couple, both special education teachers, applied to adopt a mentally retarded three-year-old black child. The child, who had been in foster care with this same white family since birth, was denied to the requesting white couple on racial grounds. The county Department of Social Services admitted that even after repeated attempts to recruit a black family, none had expressed an interest in the child. Nonetheless, the department maintained that it must continue searching. This insistence on the part of the supervisor to continue the search for an acceptable black family was in violation of the Code of Maryland Regulations, which states, "The race or national descent of prospective adoptive parents need not be the same as the adoptive child."[20] The policy interpretation of this code was that

> Every child has the right to be raised by a family of the same racial background. Therefore local departments shall never consider a transracial placement until at least the following efforts have been made and have failed to produce an appropriate adoptive family of the same race as the child.[21]

The "efforts" referred to in the policy interpretation include local and statewide recruitment of racially similar families, referral among local agencies, and use of regional and national adoption exchanges. (An American Civil Liberties Union attorney, who represented the white adoptive family in question, referred to these policies as unconstitutional and racially discriminatory.)[22] No acceptable black family was located.[23] Meanwhile the child was allowed to remain in the foster home.

In defense of the county's ruling, the director of children's welfare services stated, "It is our belief—supported by professional studies—that a child must have access to its culture."[24] The statement that "professional studies [indicate] that a child must have access to its culture" is more a reflection of this individual's personal values than it is an empirical determination—a "hope" rather than an actual assessment. The adoption supervisor was further quoted as saying that both transracially and intercountry adopted children have more emotional problems (than, one would assume, "ordinary," e.g., nonadopted, children).[25] There are currently no scientific data that support the above statement by the county adoptive supervisor. This statement exemplifies the commonly held belief that TRA will not work. Our data indicate that although many transracially adoptive parents do not go to any special lengths to emphasize their children's cultural identity, there are some who make a special effort to do so. Furthermore, even if adoptive parents do not vigorously and repeatedly reinforce the cultural identity of their nonwhite children, their action—or inaction—is not tantamount to a denial of their culture.

Following publication in the *Baltimore Sun* of the attempt at transracial adoption described at the beginning of this chapter, a series of follow-up articles, editorials, letters to the editor, and "human interest" stories appeared not only in the *Sun* but nationally as well.[26] The overwhelming majority, if not all, spoke in favor of cross-racial adoption. Of particular interest was a syndicated piece by Carl T. Rowan. In a column entitled "Should Whites Adopt a Black?" Rowan eloquently argued against the "abominable notion that race must be the dominant factor in deciding who can deliver loving care and protection to a child." Rowan equated the position of those black social workers supporting only inracial black adoption with a 1954 statement by a Mississippi editor that "every child has the right to be educated among children, and by teachers, of the same racial background."[27]

Approximately one month after the white couple petitioned to adopt the three-year-old black child, they received custody, and several weeks later the county's advisory board to the Department of Social Services proposed new policies that reduced the importance of racial factors in adoption. Although the tentative policies continued to stress that social workers should make efforts to locate racially similar adoptive parents for children, "other parents of different racial, cultural, religious or ethnic background will not be excluded, however, while a brief search for appropriate parents is conducted."[28] In discussing the proposed policy change, the county director of social services said that it clarifies "our values when dealing with children of different racial, religious, ethnic or cultural backgrounds."[29]

The last act in this particular controversy occurred in January 1985, when a black state senator proposed legislation that prohibited state agencies from blocking adoptions primarily on the basis of race: "Where a good interracial adoption possibility exists it is important that the government is not placed in the position of delaying or interfering with the best interests of the child."[30]

But the controversy over transracial adoption did not end when this one white family in Baltimore County, Maryland, received custody of a three-year-old black child and a bill was introduced in the Maryland legislature that prohibited state agencies from interfering with interracial placement solely on racial grounds. In their *NASW News*, the National Association of Social Workers (NASW) quoted a social worker familiar with the case as stating that the child in question could have been placed with a black family had the county pursued available resources.[31] According to the NASW, a black social worker in neighboring Washington, D.C., indicated that several black families had expressed an interest in the child but were turned away. Additionally, several adoption agencies in the Washington area (with, one would assume, large black constituencies) also maintained that they could have placed the child with a black family had they been approached. Finally, an interracial couple, according to the article, had expressed an interest in the child two years prior to this entire series of events but were never contacted by the county adoption agency.

Some black professionals argue that a major bottleneck in the placement of black children in black adoptive homes is caused by the predominantly white child welfare agencies staffed mainly by white social workers, who exercise control over adoptions. The fact that these white agencies are in the position of recruiting and approving black families for adoption causes some blacks to insinuate that there is institutional racism on the part of whites. In contrast, there have been several instances where concerted efforts by black child welfare agencies to locate and approve adoptive black families resulted in the adoption of comparatively large numbers of parentless black children. For example, in a recent single year Homes for Black Children, located in Detroit, placed 132 black children in black homes, more than all the other 13 child welfare agencies in Detroit combined in the same year. Similarly, when Illinois began to utilize community media in the Chicago area, in combination with simplifying the adoption procedure, the number of "special needs" adoptions increased by 70 percent in 15 months.[32] It would thus seem that if there were a backlog of approved black families waiting for black children, the entire issue of adoption across racial lines would be moot. The fact that this has not occurred—there is not a sufficient number of approved black families—is taken as evidence that whites would rather have a black child adopted by a white family than a black family.

The above position was strongly argued by Evelyn Moore, executive director of the National Black Child Development Institute. In an extensive interview on the child welfare system published by the NASW in April 1984, a significant part of which dealt either directly or indirectly with TRA, Moore said that 83 percent of all child welfare workers in the United States are white, while 30–40 percent of their cases deal with black families.[33] This skewed ratio, she contends, is one of the reasons that there are so few inracial black adoptions. "The adoption system in this country was established to provide white children to white families. As a result, most people who work in the system know very little about black culture or the black community." Moore also argues that "white middle-class standards" are largely responsible for the rejection of low and working class black families as potential adopters, who are instead encouraged to become foster parents. "While black children under the age of 19 represent only 14 percent of the children in America, they represent 33 percent of all children not living with their birth parents" (e.g., in foster care or institutionalized).[34]

Two National Urban League studies are cited by black professionals and organizations as further evidence of the likelihood that institutional racism is one of the primary reasons that more black children are not given to prospective black adoptive families. These studies reported that of 800 black families applying for adoptive parent status, only 2 families were approved (one-quarter of 1 percent), as compared to a national average of 10 percent.[35] Another study concluded that 40–50 percent of black families sampled would consider adoption.[36] An acceptance rate of one-quarter of 1 percent becomes somewhat more dramatic when compared to black inracial adoption rates of 18 per 10,000 families (figures for whites and Hispanics are 4 and 3 per 10,000 families, respectively).[37]

How can one explain the discrepancy between the apparently widespread desire to adopt among blacks and a dearth of approved black homes for adoption? We believe the answers have not changed appreciably since the publication of our first study in 1975. First of all, blacks have not adopted in the expected numbers because child welfare agencies have not actively recruited in black communities using community resources, the black media, and churches. Second, there is a historic suspicion of public agencies among many blacks, the consequence of which is that many restrict their involvement with them. Third, many blacks feel that no matter how close they come to fulfilling the criteria established for adoption, the fact that many reside in less affluent areas makes the likelihood of their being approved slight.

The intransigent opposition of most major black social work organizations to transracial adoption may be seen in a recent statement by the president of the National Association of Black Social Workers (NABSW): "We're trying to maintain our racial identity. The United States is not a melting pot. It has never been, and it's not going to be. I believe Jewish kids should be raised by Jewish parents, Indian kids should be raised by Indian parents, and so forth."[38] In 1972, referring to TRA, the NABSW said, "Black children should be placed only with black families, whether in foster care or for adoption." The statement was issued in order "to end this particular form of genocide."[39]

The recent statement by the NABSW indicating that "the United States is not a [racial] melting pot" is supported by most interpreters of the 1980 census. Herbert Gans, for example, in commenting on the rates of intermarriage reported in the census, stated, "If you're talking about the melting pot, on the whole we are a melted society.... ethnicity isn't very important anymore, and race is terribly important."[40] Similarly, a psychologist investigating children of intermarriage said, "The melting pot has melted only so far.... rates of intermarriage may have changed, but prejudices haven't."[41]

Without denying the importance of race to many Americans, the individuals and families in our study, particularly the transracially adopted children, represent a different and special cohort, one socialized in two worlds and therefore perhaps better prepared to operate in both. The hope is that having had this unique racial experience, they will have gained a greater sense of security about who they are and will be better able to negotiate in the worlds of both their biological inheritance and their socialization.

NOTES

1. Robert A. Erlandson, "Maryland Interracial Policy Impedes Adoption Attempt," *Baltimore Sun*, July 11, 1984, p. 1.

2. Ibid.

3. Ibid.

4. Ibid.

5. William Feigelman and Arnold Silverman, *Chosen Children: New Patterns of Adoptive Relationships* (New York: Praeger, 1983).

6. Glenn Collins, "Children of Intermarriage," *New York Times*, June 20, 1984, p. C1.

7. Glenn Collins, "A New Look at Intermarriage in the United States," *New York Times*, February 11, 1985, p. C13.

8. "Families Adopting Children Everywhere," *FACE Facts* 9, no. 5, (April 1985): 7.

9. Penelope L. Maza, "Adoption Trends: 1944–1975," *Child Welfare Research Notes #9.* (Washington, D.C.: Administration for Children, Youth, and Family, August 1984).

10. Christine Bachrach "Adoption Plans, Adopted Children, and Adoptive Mothers: United States, 1982 [Working Paper #22.]" U.S. Department of Health and Human Services, Public Health Service, Office of Health Research, Appendix II.

11. Maza, op. cit.

12. Michael Gold, "The Baby Makers," *Science '85* (April 1985).

13. Ibid.

14. Penelope Maza, "What We Do and Don't Know about Adoption Statistics," *Child Welfare League of America* 3, no. 2 (Spring 1985): 5.

15. Rita J. Simon and Howard Altstein, *Transracial Adoption: A Follow-up* (Lexington, Mass.: Lexington Books, 1981), p. 96.

16. North American Council on Adoptable Children, *Adoptalk* (March/April 1983): 1.

17. Reflecting the 100,000–120,000 figure, *U.S. News and World Report* in June 1984 estimated about 100,000 children available for adoption (Harold Kennedy, "As Adoptions Get More Difficult," June 25, 1984, p. 62).

18. "A Place for Foster Children," *New York Times*, June 27, 1984, p. C15.

19. Bachrach, op. cit., p. 14.

20. "Race and National Descent," Code of Maryland Regulations, COMR, Title 07, Department of Human Resources, Vol. 3, Supplement 07, 1982, pp. 112–13; 04, "Approval of Adoptive Family," p. 6.

21. Erlandson, "Maryland Interracial Policy."

22. Robert A. Erlandson, "Plan Would Cut Adoption's Racial Criteria," *Baltimore Sun*, September 2, 1984, p. C2.

23. Ibid.

24. Ibid.

25. Ibid.

26. Rita J. Simon, "Adoption Across Racial Lines: A Study's Findings," *The Christian Science Monitor*, September 18, 1984, p. 16; "Adoption Across Racial Lines," *Washington Post*, July 19, 1984, p. 21; "Gray Matter," *West Palm Beach Post*, July 30, 1984, p. E1.

27. Carl T. Rowan, "Should Whites Adopt Blacks?" *Washington Post*, July 13, 1984, p. A19.

28. Erlandson, "Plan Cuts Racial Criteria."

29. Ibid.

30. "In the Legislature," *Baltimore Sun*, January 18, 1985, p. 3D.

31. "Transracial Adoptions Controversy Grows," *NASW News*, October 1984, p. 3.

32. "Black Children Facing Adoption Barriers," *NASW News*, April 1984, p. 9.

33. Ibid.

34. Ibid.

35. Ibid.

36. Ibid.

37. Ibid.

38. Ibid.

39. The National Association of Black Social Workers Conference, Nashville, TN, April 9–12, 1972, Position Paper.

40. "A Place for Foster Children," op. cit.

41. Ibid.

2
Recent Court Rulings

> A child reared in a home with parents of a different race will be apt to meet
> and want to marry a person of his or her parents' background, not its own.[1]

So read a 1954 Georgia statute which forbade transracial adoption. One might have expected that laws based solely on race would no longer be tolerated in U.S. society. In fact, recent decisions by the U.S. Supreme Court have stated that laws that consider race a factor are "inherently suspicious." The Court has also declared that the statutory use of race will be considered consitutional only if it assists the interests of the government, is necessary, and is "precisely tailored."[2]

In 1985, transracial adoption is a legal form of child placement in every state. Nevertheless, when adoptions or custody petitions are interracial, they are often denied by the court, initially or on appeal, for no other reason than race. In a 1968 law review article, Susan Grossman argued that decisions against transracial placements, based solely on the criterion of race, are a violation of the Fourteenth Amendment.[3]

> No State shall...deprive any person of life, liberty or property without due
> process of law; nor deny to any person within its jurisdiction the equal pro-
> tection of the laws.

The test of the equal protection standard is "essentially one of reasonableness; the equal protection clause requires the states to exercise their powers so as not to discriminate between their inhabitants except upon some reasonable differentiation fairly related to the object of regulation."[4] Thus, regarding TRA, the courts have been charged with the task of deciding if the use of race as a factor in adoption proceedings is reasonable in light of the judicial purpose, which is to determine the best interests of the child.

This chapter reviews child custody cases in which race has been a factor in state and federal jurisdictions, primarily between 1980 and 1984. But we begin our discussion with a 1973 case that was argued in the Pennsylvania Supreme Court, because the findings of that case are cited in numerous other child custody decisions in which race was considered an important element in the court's ruling.

In *Lucas v. Kreischer*, the Pennsylvania Supreme Court overturned a 1971 ruling by the Court of Common Pleas which awarded three white children to the custody of their biological father.[5] The mother was allowed visitation privileges. Briefly, the facts of the case are as follows. Immediately after the separation the children lived with their mother for a brief period. Then, the mother consented to an arrangement whereby the children stayed with their paternal grandparents until she found adequate housing. During the time the mother was looking for housing, the children moved from their paternal grandparents' home to their father's home. After a brief period of time the father requested that the mother agree to have the children live with her, which she did. At that time she was sharing an apartment with a black man. Shortly after their divorce both parents remarried, the father to a white woman and the mother to the black man with whom she had been living. At some point in the same month that the mother remarried, the children's father asked for and received permission from his former wife to take the children to his home for a visit. He then refused to return them. The mother petitioned for their return in the Court of Common Pleas. In awarding custody to the father, a majority of the court stated that although the biological mother and her husband were "fit persons to have custody of the children...[the children would be near certain casualties of the] almost universal prejudice and intolerance of interracial marriage."[6]

An interesting dissenting opinion was then filed.[7] In speaking of racial intermarriage, the opinion quoted the lower court: "This bias, however silly and unreasonable, is also exhibited toward the children (of interracial marriages); and it must be admitted the plight of these children in the past has not been a happy one and in our opinion, this ancient phobia merits consideration in this case."[8] It was on the basis of this "ancient phobia" that the lower court rendered its decision and not, as the dissenting opinion argued, on the "presumption that children of tender years should remain with their natural mother"—a rule of law so ingrained and generally accepted as to be almost a given. Additionally, the dissenting opinion strongly argued that

the "separate but equal" racial doctrine was condemned a decade ago in Brown v. Board of Education. Subsequent decisional law has made it axiomatic that no State can directly dictate or casually promote a distinction in the treatment of persons solely on the basis of their color. To be within the condemnation, the governmental action need not effectuate segregation of facilities directly. The result of the statute or policy must not tend to separate individuals by reason of difference in race or color. No form of State discrimination, no matter how subtle, is permissible under the guarantees of the Fourteenth Amendment freedoms.[9]

In its conclusion, the dissenting opinion stated: "In a multiracial society such as ours, racial prejudice and tension are inevitable. If these children are raised in a happy and stable home, they will be able to cope with prejudice and hopefully learn that people are unique individuals who should be judged as such."[10]

The Pennsylvania Supreme Court reversed the lower court's decision, stating: "The real issue posed by this appeal is, whether a subsequent interracial marriage by the mother, in and of itself, is such a compelling reason as will warrant a court in denying her the custody of her children. We rule it is not."

In 1980, the ruling in the Iowa case of *Kramer v. Kramer* began to limit the use of race as a factor in child custody.[11] A divorcing white couple were disputing the custody of their two minor children. The court considered it relevant that shortly after the couple separated, the husband returned to the family home and found a black man sleeping on the couch. The wife stated that she had had sexual relations with the man and that he had moved to the couch when the daughter had come into the bedroom. She stated that she had had sexual relations with the man on two or three occasions. At the time of the divorce trial, she testified that she had not seen the man for over five weeks and that she had no intentions of marrying him. The court stated that to allow a "biracial relationship...to exist in the presence of the children is not in their best interest and is going to make their lives in the future much more difficult."[12] Custody of the children was awarded to their father.

The Supreme Court of Iowa, upon appeal, ruled that "the trial court erred in basing its custody decision on racial considerations" and that race cannot be a decisive factor in questions of custody.[13] The custody award remained with the father, however, because the court found the mother's emotional instability a more compelling reason not to reverse the original custody decree.

In addition to ruling on the specifics of that case, the *Kramer* decision began to develop an outline for "reasonable" uses of racial considerations in adoption decisions. The outline provided by the *Kramer* court stated:

1. Unsubstantiated judicial predictions concerning the effects of racial prejudices in the community are not to dictate the disposal of child custody issues.
2. Child custody decisions shall not be affected by the existence of racial tension unless it can be clearly demonstrated that this tension is relevant to the decision.
3. Simply proving the existence of racial tension or prejudice in the community is not sufficient to show relevancy.

4. Even when race is proven to have some demonstrated relevancy, the factor of race should serve only as one consideration, to be weighed together with all other considerations.

5. The proof that race is relevant to a child custody decision must be garnered from the evidence specific to each particular case.

Another 1980 case involved a dispute between two white parents over custody of their minor daughter.[14] The court found relevant that the mother planned to marry a black man. It then predicted continuous adjustment difficulties for the child if she were to live with parents of differing races and awarded custody to the father.

The decision was appealed and the appellate court determined that in establishing the best interests of the child, race should be ignored as a factor. In its decision the court wrote:

> There has been a marked increase in the United States in recent years of interracial marriages and transracial adoptions, and sociological studies establishing that children raised in a home consisting of a father and a mother who are of different races do not suffer from this circumstance.[15]

This statement, which acknowledged that transracial adoptions cause no detrimental effects to a child's welfare, supported the growing judicial proposition that the use of race as a factor is unreasonable and should not be allowed.

In another Iowa case heard in 1980, race played an important but less crucial role than in the two decisions cited above.[16] The relevant facts are as follows:

After seven years of marriage, a white couple gave birth to a son. Approximately four years later they adopted two biracial infants, a boy and a girl born one year apart, each with one black parent. Ten years after the transracial adoption, the couple divorced. They agreed that all three children should remain with the mother and that the father should pay child support and have visitation rights. Eight months after the divorce, with both parents' consent, the biological son returned to his father's home, leaving the two transracially adopted children with their mother. With the mother's agreement, the father reduced his child support by one-third. The father then petitioned in district court for custody of his remaining two (transracially adopted) children, who continued to live with his former wife. One argument in his petition was that their mother "did not adequately assist them in developing a positive view of their racial identity."[17] As evidence that he would be more equipped to parent his transracially adopted children, he cited his role as a Unitarian minister, his friendships with black people, and his election to the vice-presidency of the local chapter of the National Association for the Advancement of Colored People (NAACP). The father claimed that he would be better able to help his children "associate with black persons in order to establish a sense of their own black identity and to appreciate black values."[18]

The court acknowledged that even though the children's mother did not herself have any black friends, the children did, and that, "on balance, she has done well for the children and has been a good parent."[19] In recognizing that race "is not a controlling factor in child custody adjudication,"[20] the court denied the father's appeal for custody of his transracially adopted children. It could not, however, resist bowing in the direction of the broadly accepted hesitation about the "normalcy" of this type of permanent child placement and commented:

> Impressive evidence was received concerning special problems in transracial adoptions. Black children adopted by white parents risk a loss of identity which affects their self-esteem, their ability to cope with community prejudice, and their relationship as adults with black peers. In addition, they risk being deprived of the enriching influence of black culture.[21]

In *Farmer v. Farmer*, a New York case in 1981, race was once again viewed by the court as only one factor among a host of others to be considered in rendering its decision.[22] A divorcing interracial couple (black husband, white wife) each sued for custody of their six-year-old daughter. The father's petition asserted that his daughter would be identified by American society as black—an undisputed claim—and that therefore she should be reared in a black environment which he, a black person, could provide. In arguing that his daughter would experience identity problems if awarded to her mother, he claimed that "social and psychological problems can result from the unresolved internal conflicts which are the product of confused identity."[23] One of the father's expert witnesses opined:

> What I'm trying to say, a black youngster who is raised in a black home, of course a possibility exists that the youngster will still grow up with problems. I [am] trying to put things into perspective. If I'm a black youngster raised in a black home, if I clearly know who I am, if I have all sorts of role models around me, even though there may be a number of slings and arrows thrown at me from without, at least I can sustain myself within the groups.[24]

Witnesses for the child's mother argued:

> Nurturing is the relationship between parent and child that accords the child a sense of security, stability, warmth, love, and affection.... Economic stability is valuable; emotional stability is crucial.... How the parent relates to the child, the parents' communication with the child, which includes the sharing of emotions, is crucial.... race has low priority on the scale of values

determining best interests. The color of the custodial parent is immaterial to the child. . . . this child is white as well as black and what will be important to her is how her parents' sensitivity to her will affect her.[25]

The court concluded that

race is of little or no significance where the issue is custody. . . . It is simply one of many factors which may be considered in a contest between biological parents for custody of an interracial child. . . . that the best interests of this child. . .compel the award of custody to him [the father] because society will perceive her to be black must be rejected."[26]

In another case a white mother was given custody of her son after her divorce from the child's (white) father. Two years later, in 1981, after she had given birth to an interracial daughter whose father was black, the boy was ordered removed from his mother's custody and awarded to his paternal grandmother upon the latter's petition. The mother's charge that her son was removed on racial grounds was upheld by the Georgia Supreme Court, which ordered that the boy be sent back to her. But before the child was returned to his mother, his biological father petitioned for custody, and the court found in favor of the father. The court concluded that the mother was "sexually irresponsible" and had an "unstable life-style." Not only, the court added, was her conduct with her black paramour "immoral and a bad influence on the child," but she had "failed to set an appropriate moral example." The biological father, on the other hand, had remarried a woman with two daughters. One is left to assume that the woman was white. He has "given the appearance of being a hard-working man. . .part of a wholesome family unit," said the court. "I was rejected by a good majority of the community. . . . I was rejected by the white people," countered the boy's mother, to no avail.[27]

One of the strongest statements against the use of race as a factor may be found in a 1982 Pennsylvania case, *Re Custody of Temos*.[28] The case involved a dispute between a white couple over the custody of their two minor children. In awarding custody to the father, the lower court placed considerable weight on the fact that the mother "maintained a close relationship with a married man" who was black.[29] They planned to marry, though it was not known whether this would actually occur. In its decision, the court, referring to race, wrote, "As far as we're concerned it's relevant. . . . It [race] is a factor. There are many factors to consider in a child custody matter and. . .this is a factor. It certainly may not be a determinative factor."[30]

The lower court's decision was overturned by the Superior Court of Pennsylvania. In its decision the court stated:

This was an error, of the most serious dimension. In a child custody case, race is not a "consideration," or "concern," or "factor." Questions about race are in no respect "appropriate." In stating that race "ought to be a" consideration, the lower court was fundamentally mistaken.

A court may not assume that because children will encounter prejudice in one parent's custody, their best interests will be served by giving them to the other parent. If the children are taunted and hurt because they live with a black man, with love and help they may surmount their hurt and grow up strong and decent—the sort of children any parent would be proud of.

We know that may not happen. No feature of our society, neither religious intolerance nor economic greed, is more damaging than racial prejudice. Perhaps the children will not surmount their hurt. But a court must never yield to prejudice because it cannot prevent prejudice. Let the court know that prejudice will condemn its award; it must not trim its sails. Coke said it best: God send me never to live under the law of Convenience or Discretion.

A court should declare the law. If the court frames its decree in consideration of convenience or discretion, it betrays the law. For it yields to the anticipated reaction of those who object to the law and would object to the decree if the decree declared the law. A court that yielded to considerations of convenience and discretion would not have declared that a black child may attend any public school; play at any public park; live in any neighborhood. The fundamental principle of our law is that all persons are created equal. A court's decree should always exemplify that principle.[31]

Citing the authors' previous work, a Washington, D.C., court of appeals in January 1983 overruled a 1979 superior court decision, which had denied the adoption petition of white foster parents for their two-year-old black foster daughter. The court reasoned that the concept of "identity" had at least three dimensions:

1. A sense of "belonging" in a stable family and community.
2. A feeling of self-esteem and confidence.
3. "Survival skills" that enable the child to cope with the world outside the family.

The superior court had ordered the child placed with her paternal grandparents, who had filed for adoption upon being informed of the foster parents' petition. Social workers had interviewed the competing petitioners and recommended that "based on the premise that the best place for a child is...with blood relatives," the child be placed with the grandparents. "Cross-racial adoption always will be harmful to a child and—at the very least—should be discouraged," said a psychiatrist testifying at the trial.

Overturning the superior court's decision, the court of appeals insisted that "a presumption based solely upon the race of competing sets of would-be parents has no place in adoption proceedings.... [Race is] an impermissible intellectual shortcut." On the other hand, the dissenting judge on the appellate court wrote, "Black children in interracial families may be even more exposed to racist attitudes than other blacks...their need for survival skills is more acute. White parents, however, tend to be less equipped to pass on those skills. . . . [It is] unrealistic to blind ourselves to color in such instances."[32]

In _Miller v. Berks County Children and Youth Services,_ a Pennsylvania case decided in 1983, race was a secondary but powerful factor in the court's decision. Pennsylvania law states that the

> paramount concern in all custody cases is best interest and permanent welfare of the child; all other considerations are deemed subordinate to the child's physical, intellectual, moral and spiritual well-being. . . . the. . . racial . . . background of the child shall decide its desirability on the basis of the physical, mental and emotional need and welfare of the child.[33]

In _Miller,_ an 83-year-old farmer and his 75-year-old wife parented a biracial boy (black mother, white father) from the time he was three days old until he was four years old, when he returned to his natural mother, a young black woman who had also been parented by the elderly white couple. She was living with a Caucasian man who was the father of her twins. The twins, the boy in question, his mother, and her paramour were all living together. The elderly couple asked for and received visitation and intermittent custody rights. After the murder of the child's mother by the twins' father, an act witnessed by all three children, the couple obtained temporary custody of the child. A court then awarded the boy to the county children and youth service, after deciding that the couple were not legal custodians. All three children were then placed in a black foster home (the foster mother age 39, the foster father less than 50), with summer and weekend visitation rights given to the white couple. The lower and superior courts rejected the couple's petition to have the boy returned.

Three legal statements published in 1984 and 1985 conclude this discussion: a decision by the U.S. Supreme Court upholding interracial placements; an article in the _Notre Dame Law Review_ arguing against transracial adoption; and a case pending before the courts at the time of writing. Each is described briefly.

In February 1984, the U.S. Supreme Court, despite its traditional avoidance of litigation involving domestic arguments, reluctantly heard _Palmore v. Sidoti._[34] The Court emphasized its usual procedure concerning domestic cases: "The judgment of a state court determining or reviewing a child custody decision is not ordinarily a likely candidate for review by this Court."[35] _Palmore v. Sidoti_ encapsulated all the controversies and processes historically identified with child custody when the racial identity of any family member is a factor. The child of a divorcing white couple was awarded to her mother, who entered into a relationship with a black man whom she subsequently married. The child's father petitioned for custody of his daughter, citing the mother's marriage. The court agreed with the father even though "there is no issue as to either party's devotion to the child, adequacy of housing facilities, or respectability of the new spouse of either parent.''[36] It then somewhat paradoxically continued:

> This court feels that despite the strides that have been made in bettering relations between the races...it is inevitable that [the child] will, if allowed to remain in her present situation and attains school age and thus more vulnerable to peer pressures, suffer from the social stigmatization that is sure to come.[37]

The child's mother appealed to the Supreme Court. Acknowledging that the lower court established the competency of either parent to care for their daughter, the Court rejected the father's plea that custody should revert to him. The Court additionally recognized the lower court's exclusive use of race as a determining factor, in favor of the father. In reversing the decision, the Court stated:

> A core purpose of the Fourteenth Amendment was to do away with all governmentally-imposed discrimination based on race. Classifying persons according to their race is more likely to reflect racial prejudice than legitimate public concern; the race, not the person, dictates the category....
>
> Whatever problems racially-mixed households may pose for children in 1984 can no more support a denial of constitutional rights than could the stresses that residential integration was thought to entail in 1917. The effects of racial prejudice, however real, cannot justify a racial classification removing an infant child from the custody of its natural mother found to be an appropriate person to have such custody.[38]

Clearly, the developments in 1984 did not end the controversies surrounding child placement when there are racial differences among the participants. Indeed, one wonders what it will take to convince lower courts that when race alone is defined as a significant factor in deciding child custody, those decisions are overturned on appeal. As the Supreme Court indicated in *Palmore v. Sidoti*, ''Reality of private biases and possible injury they might inflict are not permissible considerations under the equal protection clause.''[39]

Writing in the *Notre Dame Law Review*, Margaret Howard argued strongly against placing nonwhite children into white adoptive homes.[40] Admitting that the number of parentless nonwhite children exceeds the availability of nonwhite families willing to accept them, Howard urged: ''The alternative to transracial adoption...is not inracial adoption but non-adoption, i.e., continued institution or foster care.''[41] She stated:

> If the goal is to maximize the possibility of healthy emotional growth, then our best information tells us that a stable family is of paramount importance,

and the transracial placement should be made. If, however, cultural identity is more important, then transracial adoption should not be permitted.[42]

And in conclusion, Howard posited: "There is very little to recommend transracial adoption—except that the alternatives are so often worse."[43]

In spite of all the courts' decisions and precedents, the issue of race in child custody remains as powerful an influence today as at any other time. For example, in 1985 in Detroit, Michigan, when white foster parents wanted to adopt their 17-month-old biracial (black-white) foster daughter with Down's syndrome, who had been placed in their home at the age of one month, the county Department of Social Services dissuaded them on the grounds that racial matching of children and adoptive parents is a significant factor in the child's later adjustment. The foster parents were also told that the child "had the racial identity of her 'non-Caucasian' parent."[44] After seeing the child's picture in the newspaper, a black couple filed a petition for adoption and was selected in a competition with 15 other families. Upon petition by the foster parents, the court ordered that the adoption should be postponed until the Department of Social Services could complete an investigation as to which couple would be the most suitable adoptive family. The county circuit court awarded temporary custody of the child to the foster parents pending a recommendation to the probate court by the Department of Social Services.

A second case also involved litigation initiated by white foster parents when social workers abruptly removed a two-and-a-half-year-old black child from their care solely because they were white. The child had been with them since the age of 14 months, having been in seven prior foster homes.[45] The foster parents sued the State Department of Social Services for "invidious racial discrimination."[46] The American Civil Liberties Union (ACLU) joined the suit on the grounds that the department's policy of racial matching was unconstitutional. The court ordered the child returned to the foster parents. The judge described the department's policies as "absolutely and utterly absurd."[47]

These cases once again bring to the surface all the passions regarding cross-racial placement of parentless children. Two decades of research into various aspects of transracial adoption by several investigators in different parts of the United States, using different populations, have for the most part found no adverse effects to any individual or group. Yet despite these findings, stereotypical opposition to transracial adoption seems to prevail at almost all levels of the social service system.

Most of the cases described in this chapter adhered to what is by now a familiar pattern. As part of the settlement in a divorce case, a lower court awards a white child to one of its biological parents (usually the mother). The mother subsequently enters a relationship with a black man. The remaining parent challenges the original custody decision based on predicted negative consequences should the child remain in an interracial environment. An appellate court rules in favor of the noncustodial parent, accepting the argument that interracial placement is detrimental to the child. The other parent petitions a higher court to reinstate the original custody ruling and wins. A slight variation of this scenario is one in which, prior to a court's initial ruling in a divorce hearing, a divorcing parent who is seeking custody of the child (again, usually the mother) is having a relationship with a black. The other parent counters with the "predicted negative consequences" argument. The court rules against the parent who is having a relationship with a black, and an appellate court reverses that trial court's verdict.

It should be noted, however, that the courts have attempted to clarify some difficult issues regarding transracial adoptions. By and large, they have determined that race may neither serve as an automatic classification nor as a decisive and determinative factor in child custody. Judicial answers, though, still reflect ambiguity. During the 1980s, the courts have attempted to add some predictability to actual adoption practice by delineating boundaries within which decisions of a transracial nature may be made. Specifically, the decisions in *Edel, Kramer, Farmer, Temos,* and *Palmore* have taken a stand against the use of race as a factor or consideration. But the traditionally unclear rulings, which allow for discretion in agency use of racial factors still mitigate against any predictability. This lack of predictability may be seen in the fact that transracial adoptions continue to fuel legal battles.

NOTES

1. R.M.D. and E.M.D., #79-747, District of Columbia Court of Appeals, 454 A.2d, 770.
2. *Plyler v. Doe,* 102 S.Ct. 2382, 2395 (1982) Accord Dunn, supra at 343; *Zablocki v. Redhail,* 434 U.S. 374, 388 (1978).
3. Susan Grossman, "A Child of a Different Color: Race as a Factor in Adoption and Custody Proceedings," *Buffalo Law Review* 17 (1968): 303.
4. Ibid.
5. *Lucas v. Kreischer,* 450 Pa. 352, 299A.2D 243 (1973).
6. Ibid. p. 245.
7. *COM. ex rel Lucas, Aplnt. v. Kreischer* Dissenting Opinion, 221 Pa. Superior Ct. 196 (1972).
8. Ibid., p. 199.
9. Ibid., p. 201.
10. Ibid., p. 207.
11. 297 N.W. 2d, 359.
12. Ibid., p. 360.
13. Ibid., p. 362.
14. *Edel v. Edel,* 97 Michigan, App. 266.
15. Ibid., p. 273.
16. *Mikelson v. Mikelson,* Supreme Court, Iowa, 299 N.W. 2d 670.
17. Ibid., p. 672.

18. Ibid., p. 673.

19. Ibid.

20. Ibid., p. 674.

21. Ibid.

22. Sup., 439 N.Y.S. 2d 584.

23. Ibid., p. 586.

24. Ibid., pp. 586–87.

25. Ibid., p. 588.

26. Ibid., p. 589.

27. "White Who Had Mixed Race Child Again Loses Custody of Her Son," *Baltimore Sun*, March 15, 1983, p. A3.

28. 304 Pa. Superior Ct. 82, 450 A. 2d 111.

29. Ibid., p. 83.

30. Ibid., pp. 98–99.

31. Ibid., pp. 99–101.

32. DC Ct. of Appeals 454 A.2D 770.

33. RE Davis 465 A.2D 614 (Pa., 1983).

34. 104 S.Ct. 1897 (1984).

35. Ibid., p. 1881.

36. Ibid., p. 1880.

37. Ibid., p. 1881.

38. Ibid., p. 1882.

39. *Palmore v. Sidoti*, 104 Sup. Ct. 1897 (1984).

40. Margaret Howard, "TRA: Analysis of the Best Interests Standard," *Notre Dame Law Review* 59 (1984): 503.

41. Ibid., p. 535.

42. Ibid., p. 548.

43. Ibid., p. 555.

44. "Couples' Fight to Adopt Down's Syndrome Girl," *New York Times*, February 28, 1985, C11.

45. Jan Daugherty, "State Agrees to Interracial Adoptions," *Detroit Free Press*, May 4, 1986, p. 1A.

46. Ibid.

47. Shella Gruber, "Agreement Seeks an End to Foster Bias," *Detroit News*, May 4, 1986, p. 1A.

Part II

3

Looking Back
at the Families

The research described in this book began in 1972 when we contacted 206 families living in five cities in the Midwest who were members of the Open Door Society and the Council on Adoptable Children, and asked them whether we could interview them about their decision to adopt a nonwhite child. All but 2 of the families agreed to participate in the study. The parents allowed a two-person team to interview them in their home for 60 to 90 minutes at the same time that each of their children who were between three and eight years old was being interviewed for about 30 minutes.

Seven years later we sought out these families again and were able to locate 71 percent of them. This time we interviewed only the parents by mail and telephone. In the fall of 1983 and the winter of 1984, the families were contacted a third time, when we returned to our original research design and conducted personal interviews in the respondents' homes, including the parents and the adolescent children who were still living with them.[1]

The major themes developed in this volume explain how the family members relate to each other; the racial identities of the adopted children; the adopted children's sense of integration with their families; the parents' and children's expectations concerning the future identity and bonds that the transracial adoptees (TRAs) are likely to have toward the mainly white-oriented world of their parents and siblings; and the ties that the TRAs will probably develop with the community of their racial and ethnic backgrounds, or with some composite world. We begin by briefly recounting the major findings of the first two studies.

The most important finding to emerge from our first study was the absence of a white racial preference or bias on the part of the white and nonwhite children. Contrary to other findings that had thus far been reported, the children reared in these homes appeared indifferent to the advantages of

27

being white, but aware of and comfortable with the racial identity imposed on them by their outward appearance. By and large, the parents of these children were confident that the atmosphere, the relationships, the values, and the lifestyle to which the children were being exposed would enable successful personal adjustments as adults. In writing about the results of our study in 1975, we emphasized that transracial adoption appeared to provide the opportunity for children to develop awareness of race, respect for physical differences imposed by race, and ease with their own racial characteristics, whatever they may be.

Between 1972 and 1975, transracial adoption was attacked in the strongest terms by black and native American leaders. White adoption agencies and their clients were accused of participating in cultural genocide. Sensitive to the extraordinary criticism faced by transracial adoption from the time we completed our study until the publication of the book in 1977, we commented at the end:

> If the fears expressed by black and Indian opponents of transracial adoption are realized, that these children will be white on the inside and black on the outside, and that they will be perceived by both whites and blacks as pariahs, transracial adoption will be remembered as a dismal and emotionally costly experiment. If the hopes and expectations of the parents involved in transracial adoption are realized, and their children are emotionally whole, well-adjusted, and able to move easily within and between black and white communities, society's failure to maintain and support the program will be remembered with deep regret. Time, thus, will determine transracial adoption's final evaluation.[2]

When we returned to these families in 1979, we contacted only the parents by mail and phone. We felt that it was important to have even such abbreviated contacts because most of the children were about to enter adolescence or were already young teenagers and it was a propitious time to take a second reading. We learned in 1979 that the "extraordinarily glowing, happy portrait" that we had painted seven years earlier now had some blemishes on it. It showed signs of stress and tension. We noted that

> for every five families in which there were the usual pleasures and joys along with sibling rivalries, school-related problems, and difficulties in communication between parent and child, there was one family whose difficulties were more profound and were believed by the parents to have been directly related to the transracial adoption.[3]

The serious problem most frequently cited by the parent was the adopted child's (usually a boy) tendency to steal from other members of the family. We described parents' accounts of the theft of bicycles, clothing, stereos, and money from siblings' rooms, so that brothers and sisters had resorted to putting locks on their bedroom doors. Another serious problem was the parents' rather painful discoveries that the adopted children had physical, mental, or emotional disabilities that were either genetic or the result of indifferent or abusive treatment received in foster homes.

Before describing what we learned from our interviews with the parents and their adolescent children in 1983–84, we want to describe the research design for the latest study.

Of the 133 families who participated in the 1979 study, 88 took part in the 1984 survey. In addition, 8 families who had participated in the 1972 study, but could not be found in 1979, were located in 1984 and participated. From among the 133 families who had been involved in the 1979 study, 28 had moved and could not be located; or in a few cases, when we did find them, we could not arrange to interview them. In 1 family, the only child who had been transracially adopted died in an auto accident. Eleven families declined to be interviewed; and in one city the interviewing team did not complete the scheduled interviews and we therefore lost 5 families. The refusal rate of 10 percent, while still low, was slightly higher than the 7 percent we had received in 1979.

Among the 11 families who did not wish to be interviewed, 2 of them had been divorced since 1979. The family members were separated, and some of them did not wish to "get involved." Three families had been interviewed by other researchers and felt that "enough was enough." One said, "They have gone through a number of family problems recently and this was not a good time for them." The other 5 families gave no reason. Going back to the 1979 profiles of the 11 families who declined to be interviewed in 1983–84, we found that in 5 of the families the parents described problems between them and their children. These problems included: the child had a "learning disability that put a lot of stress on the family"; the child was "hyperactive and is experiencing identity problems"; the child was "retarded and having personality problems" or had "a severe learning disability and behavioral problems that [affect] school performance"; "the adoption has not been accepted by the extended family." Another set of parents, who characterized their relations with their transracially adopted child as "negative," traced the problems to a brain injury which had resulted from an auto accident.

In five families the parents agreed to be interviewed but did not allow their children to participate for a variety of reasons; these included that only the transracially adopted children were still at home and the parents felt that they were too young (14 and 15 years old) to go through an interview that probed into the areas we were covering; that the children did not seem interested and the parents did not want to pressure them; and, in one family, that the only child still at home stated specifically that she did not want to be interviewed.

In total, the 96 families had 394 children, 213 boys and 181 girls; 256 were still living at home, and 34 were away at school but considered the parents' home their home. The others had moved away, were working, or were married. Forty-three percent of all the children had been transracially adopted.

We interviewed 218 children. They represent 55 percent of the total number of children born to or adopted by the parents and 85 percent of the children still living at home. Of the 34 children who were attending colleges or universities and considered their parents' home their official residence, we were able to interview a few because they were home on vacation. Some of the children remaining at home were too young (not yet adolescents) to be included in this phase of the study.[4] Fifty-four percent of those at home were transracially adopted. Among the transracially adopted children, we interviewed 61 boys and 50 girls, or 80 percent of those at home. Eighty-nine of the 111 TRAs are American black. The others are Korean, native American, Eskimo, and Vietnamese. We also interviewed 48 males and 43 females who were born into the families and 4 males and 12 females who are white adoptees.

The median ages of the children interviewed in the three categories were 14.9 years for the TRAs, 16.8 years for those born to the parents, and 16.9 for the same race adoptees. Their ordinal positions in the family are shown below:

Position	TRA	Born	White/Adoptee
		(Percent)	
Only child	1.0	—	—
Oldest child	7.2	35.1	31.3
Middle child	10.8	15.4	12.5
Youngest child	47.7	12.1	6.3
Other position	33.3	37.4	49.9
Total	100 (111)	100 (91)	100 (16)

In 4 of the 26 families, a transracially adopted child was the only child in the family. In 14 of the families a transracially adopted child was the oldest or the first child to join the family. In 10 of the families a white adopted child was the oldest child in the family.

At the time of the first study, the parents ranged in age from 25 to 50. The mothers' mean age was 34 and the fathers' 36. They had been married for an average of 12 years; the shortest time was 2 years and the longest was 25 years. The number of children per family ranged from one to nine, including the children born into the family as well as those adopted. Nineteen percent of the parents did not have any children born to them and described themselves as unable to bear children. Twenty-six percent of the families had adopted their first child. Since 19 percent of these parents were unable to bear children, only 7 percent of those who had children born to them had adopted their first child. Among those families who adopted more than one child (56 percent), the second adopted child occupied the "middle" position 35 percent of the time and the "youngest" position 65 percent of the time. American blacks made up the largest category of adopted children.

In 1972, none of the mothers held a full-time job outside the home. Almost all of them explained that when they and their husbands made the decision to adopt, it also involved a commitment on the wife's part to remain at home in the role of full-time mother. Before they were married, or before they had adopted their first child, 46 percent of the mothers held jobs as professionals and 3 percent had been enrolled as graduate students. About 14 percent did not work outside the home before they gave birth to, or adopted, their first child. At least 62 percent of the mothers completed four years of college, and 28 percent of them had continued on to graduate school.

Sixty-one percent of the fathers had attended university after receiving a bachelor's degree, and 68 percent worked as professionals. Most of them were ministers, social workers, or academicians. Among the remaining third, 12 percent were engaged in business, and the other 20 percent were clerical workers, sales representatives, skilled laborers, or graduate students.

The Midwest is heavily Protestant, and so were the respondents in our sample. Sixty-three percent of the mothers and 57 percent of the fathers acknowledged membership in a Protestant congregation. Lutheranism was cited as their religion by 19 percent of both mothers and fathers. Twenty-one and 22 percent of the mothers and fathers, respectively, were Catholics (which is commensurate with the national Catholic representation); 1 and 2 percent were Jewish (at least 50 percent less than the national representation). The remaining 15 to 19 percent gave no formal religious identification or affiliation. Most of the parents who stated a religious affiliation also said that they attended church regularly.

About a third of the parents described themselves as "Independent," approximately 40 percent as Democrats, and 12 percent as Republicans; the others had no preference or named a local party (in Minnesota, it was the Farmer Labor Party) as the one that they generally supported or for which they had voted in the last election.

Seventy-eight percent of the parents reported that the neighborhood in which they lived was all white. Four percent characterized it as predominantly black; and the remaining 18 percent said that they lived in a mixed neighborhood. Among the large majority who lived in an all-white neighborhood, only a few referred to that fact as inappropriate to their lifestyle since the adoption. A few were making plans to move.

We found, when we conducted the second survey in 1979, that one-third of the mothers were working full-time outside their homes. Almost all of them were engaged in professional positions of the type that they had left when they adopted their first child. We noted also that while in 1972 all of the families were intact (there had been no separations, divorces, or deaths of any of the spouses), by 1979 two of the fathers had died; in 1 family both parents had died; in 19 families the parents were divorced; and in 1 they were separated. Twenty-three families had adopted one more child since 1972, and 12 families had had another child born to them.

Seventy-seven percent of the families still lived in all-white or predominantly white neighborhoods. The others lived in "mixed" neighborhoods. Seventy-one percent of the parents reported that their children attended "mixed schools"; 6 percent said that the schools were mostly black. Sixty-three percent reported that most of their children's friends were white.

Chapters 4 through 8 in this volume describe the families' experiences between 1979 and 1984, first through the eyes of the parents and then from the perspective of the adolescents. When we had completed phase two, most of the children were just entering adolescence; during phase three almost all of them were adolescents or young adults, and 55 percent were still living at home. Chapters 4 and 5 describe the parents', and then the children's, interviews. Chapter 6 compares the responses of the parents and children on selected issues. Chapter 7 focuses on the problems, conflicts, and disappointments experienced by the families, and Chapter 8 draws a collective portrait of the typical family in the study.

NOTES

1. Most of the time, the interview team was composed of a white and nonwhite graduate student from a university located in the community in which the families lived.

2. Rita J. Simon and Howard Altstein, *Transracial Adoption* (New York: Wiley Interscience, 1977), p. 187.

3. Rita J. Simon and Howard Alstein, *Transracial Adoption: A Follow-up* (Lexington, Mass.: Lexington Books, 1981), p. 113.

4. They had been born or adopted after 1972.

4

The Parents' Story

Eighty-eight percent of both the fathers and mothers participated in the 1983-84 study. Among the remaining 12 percent, the mother served as the respondent most of the time. We found, returning to the families four and a half years after our second study, that 83 percent of the parents were still married to their original partners; six had divorced before 1979 and two after 1979. Three of the parents were separated. Half of the divorced couples had remarried. The mother had custody of the children in four families, the father in two, there was joint custody in two, and each parent had custody of at least one child in three families. In four of the families the father died, and in one family both parents died before 1979 and the children had been reared by older siblings.

The fathers' median age was 44.4 years and the mothers' 43.5 years. In 1984, 72 percent of the mothers were employed full-time outside their homes, almost all of them in technical and white-collar positions as teachers, nurses, secretaries, and so on. Sixty-six percent of the fathers continued to work in professional fields as lawyers, ministers, teachers, professors, and doctors. Most of the others were in business. The median "family" income was $44,000 (based on 92 responses). The median for the mothers was $12,000 (based on 45 responses) and for the fathers $35,000 (based on 62 responses).

The strength and form of their religious attachments remained much the same as they had been in earlier years. Of the 80 percent who designated a religious preference, 19 percent are Catholics, 2 percent are Jews, and the others are Protestants, with Lutheranism named most often by 20 percent of those who reported a religious preference. Fifty-two percent said that they went to church at least once a week. Forty-eight percent of the mothers and 46 percent of the fathers said that they prefer the Democratic over the Republican party; 53 percent of the mothers and 48 percent of the fathers described themselves as "liberals" as opposed to 8 and 16 percent, respectively, who labeled themselves "conservatives."

Ninety-three percent of the families live in single dwelling homes in residential neighborhoods. Seventy-three percent of the parents described their neighborhood as completely or almost completely white. Eighty percent of the parents reported that they had been living in the same house for at least ten years.

HOW ADOPTION CHANGED THE FAMILIES

All of the parents had made their first decision to adopt transracially at least 12 years earlier, in 1972. When we interviewed them this time, we wanted to know what aspects of their lives they lived differently as a result of their decision to adopt a child of a different race. One-third of the parents said that they did not change the pattern of their lives at all; they did nothing differently. For the rest, learning about black and native American cultures (e.g., foods, art, history, ceremonials), seeking out blacks as friends, sending their children to interracial schools, and attending black churches were the changes most of them cited that bore directly on the *transracial* aspect of their decision to adopt. But the parents also mentioned "buying a bigger house, having less discretion about moving, and having fewer outside activities."

A couple who adopted one child when they were over 40 and did not have any born to them said: "It thrust us into a younger group of people because we joined groups in which our daughter's friends' parents were involved. We also joined with them in racial protest. It totally enriched our lives." Families reported such observations as "We learned more internal tolerance." One family commented, "We spend half of our lives talking to social workers." Others reported attending black churches, taking classes in Korean cooking, attending pow-wows in the Southwest. The bottom line was: "We developed an awareness of racial issues in a white society." One family reported that they went to the Human Relations Commission because of harassment from their neighbors. They also felt as if they were "living in a fish bowl all the time." Another family remarked: "Our racial awareness preceded our decision to adopt transracially. The adoption would have never occurred if we had not had the awareness."

Parents were asked: "If you had an opportunity to start over again, what things about your living arrangements *would* you do differently after you adopted (name of first TRA child)?" Nearly half (44 percent) said that they would not have changed their lives in any significant way. The others talked about moving into a biracial neighborhood and living in a bigger house. Some parents mentioned living in a less affluent neighborhood. And one parent said: "We would not have done it. Knowing what we do today, we would not have adopted transracially."

At this stage of their lives, when most of their children were adolescents or young adults, many of the parents were not inclined to reflect on how they would have changed their lives. Perhaps it takes greater distance, more years to have elapsed after the children have left the family home and have been out on their own, before the parents are willing to contemplate and confess to what they "might have done."

Consistent with the parents' reticence to imagine a different kind of life for themselves and their children, the large majority (80 percent) claimed that the campaign waged by the National Association of Black Social Workers (NABSW) and native American groups in the early and mid-1970s against transracial adoption had bothered them, but did *not* cause them to alter their behavior or their decision to adopt a black or Indian child. Among the 20 percent who reported stronger reactions, the most common was anger at the attacks on them. Most said that they considred the NABSW arguments to be "without foundation," "a bunch of bullshit"; "it was wrong because it resulted in children not being adopted." One family told us, "When we tried to adopt a second black child, we were told 'forget it.' We then adopted A, who is Puerto Rican." Another said, "What parents can offer is so much better than what our daughter would have have had—a home instead of an institution or going from one foster home to another." Yet another set of parents admitted that their decision not to adopt another black child was a result of the campaign: "We are not sure we would have adopted had we been exposed to their arguments earlier. We decided not to adopt a third child as a result of the stance of the Black Social Workers." Others said that the attacks on them made them feel guilty. But the position of the NABSW also had the effect of strengthening their desire to know people of different races and to think more about race.

Only 8 percent of the parents thought the campaign had any effect on their adopted children. Those who did said that the children shared their anger at what they viewed as the unfairness and the wrongheadedness of the attacks. One parent said, "If anything, it made us more secure because we talked about ethnic and racial backgrounds much more than we would have if the Black Social Workers had not launched their attack."

When we first encountered these families in 1972, 75 percent of the parents claimed that they were taking "various" actions in order to have their adopted children learn about and identify with the race into which they were born. The most common efforts involved bringing books, pictures, toys, and music into their homes, along with cultural artifacts associated with or helpful in describing the child's race. One family participated in the National American Culture School located in their community by taking classes in beadwork and dancing. Their son, they told us, was a registered member of a tribe. In addition, the parents talked about their recent membership in the Open Door Society and the arrangements they made for their child to play with other nonwhite children on a regular basis.

Seven years later, in 1979, when we asked the parents essentially the same question (what efforts the parents were making to help their adopted child identify with his/her own racial group), about two-third reported much the same activities. "Roots" had been shown on television shortly before our 1979 survey, and when we encountered the families, almost all of them who had adopted a black child said that the entire family watched the program. Ten families reported that they have black godparents for their black adopted child.

Among the one-third of the families who said that they were "doing nothing," most emphasized that their lack of activity was because they did not approve of treating their adopted child as "special"—at least in the sense of catering to the child's "exotic" cultural background.

In 1984, the number of families who were still involved in activities that enhanced the racial identity of their adopted child had diminished still further. About 37 percent said that they did not do anything special; an additional 13 percent said that they used to engage in various activities, but gave them up several years ago. The rest of the families, about half of those whom we interviewed, described such activities as church attendance (in primarily black churches), observance of special holidays (e.g., Martin Luther King's birthday), black friends, music, books, and food that highlighted the children's racial heritage. One father told us that he was a clergyman and he devoted a portion of his time to serving a biracial church. Another family encouraged their children to celebrate Black History Month and to read the works of W.E.B Du Bois, Paul Robeson, and other black leaders. They also went to a black dentist. One family sent their adopted black son to an all-black private school.

Almost all of the parents (85 percent of them) believed that their transracially adopted children had some knowledge of and appreciation for their racial and ethnic background. They gained them mostly from books, courses in school, and television. Friends and participation in "ethnic activities" were thought by the parents to be much less important. Almost all of the parents (87 percent) said that they and their children discuss racial issues, attitudes, and instances of racial discrimination over the dinner table and in other informal settings, usually in the context of the children's friends, some event they had seen on television or read about in the newspaper, the activities of a political figure, and so on.

PARENTS' PERCEPTIONS OF CHILDREN'S ACADEMIC PERFORMANCE AND ASPIRATIONS

We asked the parents about the average grades that each of their children received in school last year, about their children's education and career plans, and about their reactions to those plans.

We first discuss the average grade reported by parents for their oldest child who was still living at home or who was attending college or university and for whom the parents' home remained the official residence. In 2 of the 18 families in which the oldest child was transracially adopted, the child was no longer in school. Fifteen of the remaining 16 were attending high school or junior high: the other was an undergraduate. In 9 of the 66 families in which the oldest child was born into the family, the child was no longer in school. Of the remaining 57, 36 were in college, and 21 were in high school or junior high. In 3 of the 10 families with a white adoptee as the oldest child, the child was not in school, and 2 of the remaining 7 were in college. The other 5 were in high school or junior high.

The grades shown below are culled from all the schools attended by the children.

Average Grades Among Oldest Children by Race and Adoptive Status

	TRA	Born	White/Adoptee
Mean Grade*	2.5	1.8	2.7**

*A = 1; B = 2; C = 3; D = 4; F = 5.
**Based on an N of 7.

The parents reported poorer grades for the oldest adopted (transracial and white) child than for the oldest child born into the family.

A nearly identical pattern prevailed for the second child in the family who was still at home. Eight families were not involved because they did not have more than one child at home. Forty-eight of the families had a TRA child as their second child still at home. Thirty-four families had a child who had been born to them, and six had a white adopted child. Seven families—three in the TRA category, three in the born, and one in the white adopted category—reported that the child was not in school. Twelved of the 34 parents in the born category said that their son or daughter was attending college or university, compared to one in the TRA category and none in the white adopted. The mean grades reported by the parents in the three categories for the second child are shown below.

Average Grades Among Second Oldest Children by Race and Adoptive Status

TRA	Born	White/Adoptee
2.6	1.8	2.0*

*Based on an N of 6.

The pattern is similar to that described for the oldest child in that the parents report higher grades for the child born into the family than do parents in the other two categories. Looking at the 39 families who had a TRA as their third child and at the 23 families whose third child at home was born to them, we see that again the parents report higher grades for the child born into the family.

**Average Grades Among Third Oldest
Children by Race and Adoptive Status**

TRA	Born	White/Adoptee
2.7	2.1	—*

*There were no such families.

Almost all of the children who were still in high school or junior high planned to go on to college. In discussing their oldest child who was still at home, 13 out of the 15 parents of the TRAs said that their son or daughter had plans to go on to college, as did all 21 of the children born into families and all 5 of the parents of white adoptees. The parents in almost all instances said that they agreed with the education and career plans of their children. No major differences concerning future education were reported on the basis of the adopted status or race of the child.

In addition to asking the parents to report the average grades, education levels, and educational aspirations of the children still at home, we also asked them to describe the activities in which their children like to engage and which they do well, whether they are leaders or followers, good mixers, have stable friendships, and the racial characteristics of their children's friends and dates.

Regarding the children's favorite activities and those which the parents perceived them doing well, sports was clearly the favorite for all three groups, followed by music and socializing with friends. The parents also saw their children doing best in sports. As the percentages in Table 4.1 indicate, there are no big differences among the three categories of children save that the parents perceived the oldest child born to them as having more academic and intellectual interests.

The same pattern emerged on those activities which the parents believed the children were doing well.

We report next on the socializing skills and leadership qualities the parents perceive their children as having, and about the stability of their friendships. (See Table 4.2.) Specifically, we asked:

Is (name of child) a good mixer? Or does he/she prefer to spend time alone?
Among (name of child)'s friends, is he/she a follower or a leader?
Does (name of child) keep friends over a long period of time?

Table 4.1: Favorite Activities by Race, Adoptive Status, and Ordinal Position in Family

Favorite Activities	TRA			Born			White/Adoptee		
	1st	2nd	3rd	1st	2nd	3rd	1st	2nd*	3rd*
				(in percent)					
Sports	41	55	36	23	48	47	33	--	--
Music	10	13	7	13	12	11	12	--	--
Social Activities	13	11	11	10	4	16	16		
Academic, Intellectual	10	6	--	20	8	--	--		
Arts/Crafts	--	--	11	10	--	--	8		
Other	26	15	35	24	28	26	31		
Total	100	100	100	100	100	100	100	--	--

*N's were too small.

With little difference by ordinal position or adoptive status, most parents perceive their children as "good mixers" and not as loners. But again, the responses about the oldest child born into the family are somewhat different. The oldest is more likely to be perceived as a loner than are children in any of the other categories.

As the percentages in Table 4.3 show, parents are more likely to see their children as leaders than as followers, and they are more likely to see the old-

Table 4.2: Socializing Skills by Race, Adoptive Status, and Ordinal Position in Family

Child Is a Good Mixer	TRA			Born			White/Adoptee		
	1st	2nd	3rd	1st	2nd	3rd	1st	2nd*	3rd*
				(in percent)					
Yes	72	72	76	54	76	95	67	--	--
No, loner	14	13	7	25	16	--	18	--	--
Both	10	13	3	13	--	--	8	--	--
Neither	4	2	14	8	8	5	7	--	--
Total	100	100	100	100	100	100	100	--	--

*Frequencies are too small.

Table 4.3: Leader vs. Follower by Race, Adoptive Status, and
Ordinal Position in Family

Leader/ Follower	TRA 1st	2nd	3rd	Born 1st	2nd	3rd	White/Adoptee 1st	2nd*	3rd*
				(in percent)					
Leader	48	45	61	58	52	50	38	--	--
Follower	34	32	25	19	16	22	23	--	--
Both	11	13	11	19	16	22	16	--	--
Neither	8	10	3	4	16	6	23	--	--
Total	100	100	100	100	100	100	100	--	--

*N's are too small.

est child born into the family as a leader than the children in the adoptive
categories or other ordinal positions.

Concerning the stability of their children's friendships, there was practically no variation: between 75 and 100 percent of the parents reported that
their children maintained friendships over a long period of time.

When asked about friendships and dating, the majority of all the parents
reported that their children's friends were white. But among the TRAs, they
also noted that a substantial minority had only black friends or both black and
white friends. Among the white children (those born as well as those adopted)
the percentage of parents reporting that they had only black friends was between 0 and 4. (See Table 4.4.)

Many of the parents claimed that their children did not date; they were
too young. For example, half of the parents describing their oldest TRA who
was still at home said that the child was not into dating, nor were one-third
of the oldest children born into the family or 40 percent of the white adoptees. For the second and third children, the percentages of those not dating
were higher (e.g., 70 percent among the TRAs and 52 percent among those
born into the families). We report the racial characteristics of the dates only
for the oldest TRA child and for the oldest child born into the family still living at home. (See Table 4.5.)

Focusing next on relations among family members, we asked the parents
to evaluate their relationship with each child in the family who was still living at home or was away at school but who considered the parental home to

Table 4.4: Racial Characteristics of Friends by Race, Adoptive Status, and Ordinal Position

Racial Groups To Which Friends Belong	TRA 1st	2nd	3rd	Born 1st	2nd	3rd	White/Adoptee 1st	2nd*3rd*
				(in percent)				
Only white friends	72	53	46	87	92	80	77	-- --
Only black friends	14	17	18	--	4	--	--	-- --
Black and white friends	10	23	25	10	4	10	15	-- --
Other	4	7	11	3	--	10	8	-- --
Total	100	100	100	100	100	100	100	-- --

*N's are too small.

be their own home. The rating options were (1) = the relationship is basically positive and good; (2) = there are problems but the positive elements outweigh the negative ones; (3) = the problems are such that the negative elements outweigh the positive ones; and (4) = the relationship is basically negative and bad.

On a scale of one to four, the ratings for the separate categories looked like this:

Parents' Ratings of Their Relations with Their Children

Child's Status	Mean Score
First TRA	1.57
Second TRA	1.44
Third TRA	1.57
First child born	1.30
Second child born	1.30
Third child born	1.28
First white adopted	1.40
Second white adopted*	1.66

*Frequencies are too small for the third white adopted.

Table 4.5: Racial Characteristics of Dates by Adoptive Status Among Oldest Children

Race of Dates	TRA	Born
	(in percent)	
White only	72	84
Black only	14	--
Black and white	14	9
Other	--	7
Total	100	100

We note first that the scores vary more according to the adoptive status of the children than they do by their ordinal position in the family. Thus, the ratings for the oldest, second oldest, and third oldest transracially adopted children are closer to each other than are the ratings for the TRAs and children born into the family within each ordinal position. Second, the parents evaluate their relationships with the children born to them more positively than they do those with the children they adopted, be they white or nonwhite.

The main types of problems described by parents who rated the relationships "3" or "4" revolved around discipline (which they said were beyond ordinary limits). In two families, teenage transracially adopted daughters had been picked up by the police for prostitution. In seven other families, the parents reported drinking and drug problems. Only one family reported stealing by the TRA child as a problem. In the 1979 survey, by contrast, stealing from family members had been a serious problem in at least 10 percent of the families. Family problems are discussed in detail in Chapter 7.

We also assessed the parents' evaluations of the relationships among the siblings. Using the same four-point scale, we asked the parents to evaluate the relationships among the children still at home, specifically the relationships between the first adopted child and the first and second children born into the family; between the second adopted child and the first and second children born into the family; and between the first and second adopted children.[1]

The chart compares the mean scores in each of the categories described above.

Parents' Perceptions of Children's Relations with Siblings

Siblings' Relationship	Mean Score
First adopted/first born	1.54
First adopted/second born	1.44
Second adopted/first born	1.28
Second adopted/second born	1.25
Among adopted children	1.53

We note that the parents' ratings are less positive when the relationship involves first adopted children as opposed to second adoptees, and that the ordinal position of the children born to them (first or second) is less important than that of the adopted children. The parents mention jealousy, competition, and personality differences as the major sources of the problems among the children.

We also asked about each child still at home: How does (name of child) get along with his/her brothers/sisters? The results for the three categories of families are shown in Table 4.6.

In each ordinal position, the children born into the families are perceived by their parents as having better relations with their siblings than either of the children in the adopted categories; and the TRAs are thought by their parents to have better relations with their siblings than the white adoptees. The youngest children still at home in both the born-into-the-family and TRA categories are perceived by the parents as having a better relationship with their siblings than do the older children. The white adoptees (the frequency in that category is only 13) are perceived by the parents as having more difficulties with their siblings than do the TRAs or children born into the families.

The consistent message conveyed by these evaluations is that parents have more positive relations with the children born to them than they have with their adopted children; and they perceive the children born to them as getting along better with their siblings than they do their adopted children.

Focusing on "problems" that may have emerged as a function of the parents' decision to adopt transracially, we asked the parents whether they thought the children born to them experienced difficulties with peers that they (the parents) attributed to the presence of a nonwhite sibling. About the TRA child we asked: "Do you think adolescence has been more complicated or difficult for (name of child) because he/she was adopted?"

Table 4.6: Relations Among Siblings by Race, Adoptive Status, and Ordinal Position in Family

Relations With Siblings	TRA			Categories of Children Born			White/Adoptee		
	1st	2nd	3rd	1st	2nd	3rd	1st	2nd*	3rd*
	(in percent)								
All good	34	36	48	42	48	74	23	--	--
Typical love/hate with ups and downs	41	32	22	37	28	21	30	--	--
Good with some/ poor with others	25	32	30	21	24	5	47	--	--
Total	100	100	100	100	100	100	100	--	--

*The frequencies are too small.

For the children born into the families, 78 percent of the parents said that they did not believe their first born son or daughter experienced problems as a result of having a transracially adopted sibling in the family. The few who responded affirmatively mentioned teasing and name calling as the types of problems encountered. Eighty-six percent of the relevant parents did not attribute problems for the second child born into the family to a transracially adopted sibling; nor did 72 percent of the parents for the third child.

On the other hand, parents were more likely to link difficulties to their TRAs. For example, 43 percent of the parents said of their first TRA that the child's adolescence was more complicated because of the adoption. Fourteen percent of the parents described identity problems. For example, one mother explained, "Our daughter needed to get over her sense of pain because her birth parents rejected her." Another said: "B was less secure of our love and approval. He still needs a lot more reassuring." The son was in therapy at the time of the survey.

Thirteen percent of the parents talked about emotional and behavior problems. For example, one parent said: "Our daughter used to be teased by children in school who told her her birth mother was a prostitute. That hurt her a lot." Another parent observed, "He wasn't having problems because of the adoption, but because he was growing up in a white family and had no one to turn to as a role model."

Thirty percent of the parents felt that their second TRA child also experienced identity and emotional problems in adolescence because of the child's adoptive status. For example, one mother reported that her son, who had a history of stealing from members of the family, kept asking her, "Do I belong here—will it be forever?"

RACIAL IDENTITY

We turn now to the matter of the parents' expectations and perceptions of their TRA children's racial identity. We asked the parents to recall the time when they adopted their first child, and asked:

1. Did you have an identity that you wanted or expected (name of child) to assume?
2. Have those expectations changed over the years? If they have, how and why?
3. At the present time, with which racial group does (name of child) identify? Does he/she consider him/herself black, white, Korean, etc.?
4. At the present time, do you perceive (name of child) as black, white, other?

We separated the parents' responses to the first question into two categories: their descriptions of their expectations for the transracially adopted child, and for their white adopted child. Table 4.7 shows the parents' responses for the first and second transracially adopted and the first white adopted child.

The parents' responses about their first and second transracial adoptees are similar, and both are somewhat different than their responses about their white adoptees. For the latter, more of the parents (understandably) expected the child to share the family's identity. But the largest group of parents reported that they had no expectations or desires about the identity to be assumed by their adopted child. Note also that fewer parents expected their second TRA child, as opposed to their first, to share the family's identity. Perhaps the experience of having a child of another race or ethnic background in their family sensitized them to that issue.

When we directly asked whether their expectations about their transracially adopted children had changed over the years, we found that, for at least two-thirds of the parents, they had not changed. Six percent of the parents said that they had changed their expectations for their first TRA, and 10 percent for the second TRA. In both cases the parents had shifted toward a desire for their children to assume their black identity. The higher percentage for the second transracial adoptee supports the notion that the parent had become more sensitized to the importance of ethnic identity.

Responses to question 3 and 4 are shown in Tables 4.8 and 4.9.

Table 4.7: Parents' Expectations About Adopted Child's Identity

Response Categories	Categories of Children		
	1st TRA	2nd TRA	1st White/ Adopted
	(in percent)		
We wanted our child to share the family's identity	12.2	7.1	28.4
We wanted our child to identify with his/her racial and ethnic background	23.2	26.2	---
We wanted the child to be interracial	3.6	4.8	---
We had no expectations or desires about the child's identity	50.0	47.7	43.0
Other responses (e.g., Christian, physically and intellectually able, successful woman)	6.1	7.1	14.3
No answer	4.8	7.1	14.3
Total	100	100	100

Table 4.8: Parents' Perceptions About How Child Identifies Him/Herself

| Categories | Categories of Children | | |
	1st TRA	2nd TRA	White/Adoptee
	(in percent)		
Black	48.8	47.6	--
White	26.8	28.3	58
Native American	2.4	4.8	--
Asian	4.9	2.4	--
Mixed	4.9	9.6	7
None	2.4	--	7
Other	2.4	--	--
Irrelevant	--	--	7
Don't know	3.6	2.5	7
No answer	3.8	4.8	14
Total	100	100	100

Table 4.9: Parents' Current Perceptions Of Child's Identity

| Categories | Categories of Children | | |
	1st TRA	2nd TRA	White/Adoptee
	(in percent)		
Black	42.7	45.2	--
White	10.7	9.6	64
Native American	1.2	4.8	--
Asian	4.9	7.1	--
Mixed	8.5	14.3	--
None	6.1	7.1	--
Other	2.4	--	--
Irrelevant	20.8	7.1	14
No answer	2.4	4.8	22
Total	100	100	100

About 63 percent of the parents believe that their transracial adoptees identify with the ethnic/racial background of their birth, be they black, Asian, native American, or mixed. But 27 percent believe that their nonwhite children identify themselves as white. All of these children had black and white birth parents. For the white adoptees, the parents report that one child (representing 7 percent of the group) identifies himself as mixed when, according to the parents, both of his birth parents were white.

Table 4.9 describes how the parents perceive their children. We note first that roughly the same percentage of parents perceive their child as black, native American, Asian, and white (for the white adoptees) as they report for their children's assessment. What is different in the two charts is the smaller percentage of parents who perceive their black children as white. In other words, the parents, unlike the children, do not identify their children who have black and white birth parents as white. The parents are more likely to view those children as having a "mixed" identity or to consider the racial/ethnic identity as irrelevant. Thus, the data in Tables 4.8 and 4.9 indicate that the parents are not imposing (at least explicitly) a "white" identity on their "black and white" transracial adoptees.

In the study by Ruth McRoy and Louis Zurcher of 30 black children who had been transracially adopted and 30 black children who had been adopted by black parents, the parents were asked to "denote their childrens' racial background."[2] Eighty-three percent of the inracial adopted parents (black parents and black children) listed their child's background as black/black, and 17 percent as black/white. Among the white parents who adopted black children, 27 percent reported their child's racial background as black/black, 57 percent as black/white, and the other 15 percent as black/Mexican, Indian, Korean, and Latin American. McRoy and Zurcher commented that 60 percent of the TRA parents "seemed to have taken a color-blind attitude to racial differences between the adoptee and family."[3] They described these families as living in predominantly white communities and their adopted child as attending predominantly white schools. They reported that 20 percent of the transracial parents can be characterized as acknowledging the adoptees' racial identity and the need to provide black role models for them. Those parents enrolled the child in an integrated school, moved to a neighborhood on the fringes of the black community or to an integrated neighborhood or became members of a church located in the black community. Their children expressed an interest in contact with other blacks and often discussed racial identity issues with their parents and peers.[4]

Another 20 percent of the transracial families

> were likely to have adopted several black children and acknowledged that their family was no longer white but interracial. They enrolled their children in integrated schools. Racial discussions and confrontations in the home were common. The children were taught to emphasize their black racial heritage.[5]

Comparing the parents' responses in our study against the McRoy-Zurcher data, we note that even after combining all of the parents who responded "none," "irrelevant," and "no answer" to the question of how the parent identifies the child, we come up with only 31 percent who might fit the "color blind" response that is reported by 60 percent of the TRA families in the McRoy-Zurcher study. And even after including the 10 percent who said that they identify their transracial adoptee as white, we still report a smaller percentage of parents who appear to overlook the "race issue."

We asked the parents whether any of their TRA children talked to them about slurs or insults which they might have received because of their color or racial backgrounds. Sixty-five percent of the parents said that their children had told them about at least one incident. Eight percent of the parents thought their children might have encountered such experiences but chose not to talk to them about it. The incidents which were reported to the parents by their children almost always involved name calling ("nigger," "jungle bunny," "chinkman," "Pearl Harbor," "gook," etc.) by other children. One family told us that some children in school had put up a sign on the wall which read "KKK" and "Kill the Nigger Dog." The principal found out who was involved and suspended those pupils. Seven parents said that the incident related by their children involved an insulting remark by a teacher or the parent of a friend.

Almost all of the parents reacted to their child's report by discussing the experience and trying to help the child deal with it. They explained to the children that as they grew up they were likely to encounter other such experiences and some would perhaps be of a more serious nature. In those instances in which other adults were involved (parents of friends or teachers), the parents went to the school or to the home of the parent involved. On one occasion when the parent called on a mother who had pushed the son to the floor and called him "nigger," the mother's response was, "You should not have adopted a nigger." The parent did not believe that these incidents, hurt and angered as the children were by them when they occurred, were likely to leave lasting impressions or scars.

PLANS FOR THE FUTURE

Looking ahead to the future, we asked the parents for their opinions about the ties that their TRAs were likely to have as adults when they left the parental home. For example:

 When your adopted child(ren) is an adult, do you anticipate that he/she will live mostly in the community in which he/she has been reared, or will he/she seek types of communities whose racial or ethnic characteristics match his/her background?

Of those parents who had an opinion on the matter (28 percent did not), 50 percent thought that their adopted child would live in the same community as that in which they were reared (predominantly white and middle class); 22 percent believed that they would live in a mixed racial/ethnic community; 9 percent felt that they would seek out the ethnic or racial community whose characteristics matched their racial background; and 11 percent thought that the racial or ethnic composition of the community would not be an important criterion for them. The remaining 8 percent of the parents mentioned location, city size, or other physical characteristics of the community. The parents' responses for the second TRA were of the same order. Forty-eight percent thought that their children would settle in the community in which they were reared, as opposed to 20 percent who felt that "mixed" racial/ethnic communities would be their child's choice, and 32 percent said that the racial or ethnic composition would not be relevant.

We also asked:

Do you anticipate that your adopted child will marry a person whose racial or ethnic characteristics match his or hers?

Forty-six of the parents said that they could not answer the question because they did not know. Among those who were willing to venture an opinion, 44 percent believed that their TRA child would marry a person whose racial characteristics matched his or hers, and 24 percent said that since their child had grown up in a white community, the child was likely to choose a person from that community. Sixteen percent said that "race" would not be a crucial consideration in their TRA child's choice of a marital partner. The others felt that their TRA children were not likely to choose a person of their own racial/ethnic background because they had met so few of them and were unlikely to encounter many in the future; or they believed that the TRA child would marry a white person but offered no explanation.

The responses for the second TRA child were similar insofar as half of the parents for whom the question was applicable said that their child would marry a person of their own "racial or ethnic background," and the remaining parents thought that their second TRA child would marry a white person, primarily because the child had grown up in a white community.

Continuing this focus on the future, we asked about the quality of the relationship that the parents expect to have with their children after the children leave home. Using a four-point scale again, we asked whether they thought it would be (1) close, (2) fairly close, (3) fairly distant, or (4) distant. The table below describes the mean scores.

Parents' Expectations About Future Relations with Their Children

Child's Status	Mean Score*
First TRA	1.75
Second TRA	1.62
Third TRA	1.63
First child born to parents	1.40
Second child born to parents	1.71
Third child born to parents	1.56
First white adopted	1.75
Second white adopted	2.00

*The lower the score the closer the expected relationship.

Remember that when we asked the parents to describe the quality of their relations with their children at the time the study was conducted, the children born to them, in each ordinal position, received more positive ratings than did the transracially or white adopted children. We noted also that there was more variation by adopted status than by ordinal position. In the ratings shown above, the pattern is mixed. Neither adopted status nor ordinal position stands out as a significant predictor of the quality of the relationships the parents feel that they are likely to have with their children in the future. The only exception is the first child born into the family, with whom the parents expect to be closest.

As for the parents' expectations of how close the TRAs and the children born into the families are likely to be, and how close the TRAs are likely to be with each other, we note that the parents hold remarkably similar expectations for each of the five types of relationships.

Parents' Expectations About Future Relations Among Siblings

Sibling Relationships	Mean Score
First adopted/first born	2.0
First adopted/second born	2.0
Second adopted/first born	2.1
Second adopted/second born	1.8
Among adopted children	1.9

The parents do not expect the TRAs to be closer to each other than to siblings who were born to the parents. Ordinal position also seems not to affect the parents' expectations about sibling closeness.

BIRTH RECORDS

In our 1979 survey of the parents, we introduced the delicate and controversial topic of birth records. We noted in 1979 that only 4 states permitted adult adoptees to examine their original birth certificates. The other 46 states all had statutes regulating an adult adoptee's access to his or her birth records.

In the realm of federal law, the Indian Child Welfare Act of 1978 was designed to prevent denial of tribal rights to which native American adoptees may be entitled. The law granted all such adoptees over the age of 18 access to the tribal identification of their biological parents, but did not allow the release of any personal information on the identities or whereabouts of the biological parents.

At its 1979 convention, the Delegate Assembly of the NASW issued the following statement regarding open records:

> The adoptees right-to-know and the limits of confidentiality to which the parties to adoption now are subject must be addressed.
>
> The needs and right of adoptees to know their birth origins should be recognized. This right [includes] requests from adult adoptees for identifying information. . . . The social work profession, along with social agencies, has a responsibility to initiate and support appropriate changes in the law that would facilitate sharing of identifying information between adult adoptees and birth parents when both parties are in agreement.[6]

Our 1979 study included the following question to the parents:

> In the last few years there has been quite a lot of discussion about "open records." Has your adopted child(ren) asked you directly or tried to find out in any other way about his or her biological parents and family?

We reported that 40 percent of the parents said that their adopted children expressed no interest in this topic, 42 percent stated that their children expressed mild interest, and 18 percent told us that their children expressed strong interest. We also commented on the parents' own attitudes on the issue, noting that the parents' reactions were heavily in favor (by about eight to one) of the adopted children's right to know and need to find their biological parents. Nearly all of them said thay they would help their children locate information about their biological parents after they were 18 or 21 years old.

As of 1984, the states may be divided into the following categories concerning their policies vis-a-vis open records:

Confidential Records

(Records are sealed unless adult adoptee requests that his/her record be opened. Then it is left to the court to decide whether the request is for a "good cause.")

 Alaska
 Arizona
 Delaware
 District of Columbia
 Georgia
 Hawaii
 Indiana
 Iowa
 Kentucky
 Maryland
 Mississippi
 Missouri
 Montana
 New Jersey
 New Mexico
 North Carolina
 Oklahoma
 Rhode Island
 Utah
 Vermont
 Virginia
 Washington
 West Virginia
 Wyoming

Registry and Match

(Adult adoptees and birth parent(s) register. The court then serves as an intermediary in arranging for the two partners to get together.)

 Arkansas
 California
 Colorado
 Florida
 Idaho
 Illinois
 Louisiana
 Maine
 Massachusetts
 Michigan
 Nevada
 New Hampshire
 New York
 Ohio
 Oregon
 South Carolina
 South Dakota
 Texas

Search and Consent Procedures

(Adult adoptees employ the services of an agency to search for birth parents. If agency is successful, and birth parent(s) agree, the agency arranges a meeting.)

 Connecticut
 Minnesota
 Nebraska
 North Dakota
 Pennsylvania
 Tennessee
 Wisconsin

Open Records

(Adult adoptees can demand to see their record from the court.)

 Alabama
 Kansas

In this most recent survey, we asked both the parents and the adoptees about their interest in birth records. The parents were asked:

1. Has your adopted child asked you directly or tried to find out in any other way about his or her biological parent and family? If yes, please explain.
2. What is your position about revealing information concerning your adopted child(ren)'s birth parents?
3. Do you have any information about your adopted child(ren)'s birth parents that you will *not* reveal to him/her? If yes, please explain.

Table 4.10 shows the parents' responses to the first question. According to the parents, about half of the adoptees have shown no interest in their birth parents. Approximately 30 percent asked about them but expressed no desire to locate their birth parents, and about 10 percent have told their parents that they would like to try and locate them.

Seventy-two percent of the parents believe the adoptees should have access to all the information available on the birth records when the adoptee is an adult. Twelve percent said that they have already supplied their adopted children with all the information they had about the birth parents. Three percent believe that the records should remain closed. Five percent did not answer. The remaining 8 percent placed some conditions on release of the information (e.g., medical need, mutual desire).

Table 4.10: Parents Reports About Adopted Children's Interest in Birth Parents

Degree of Interest	Categories of Children*	
	1st TRA	2nd TRA
	(in percent)	
Have not asked or shown any interest	50.8	43.4
Have not asked but parents have given them information	10.2	3.3
Asked, but parents felt threatened	3.4	--
Asked about them, but show no interest in locating	26.6	31.2
Want to find one or both parents	7.3	18.8
No answer	1.7	3.3
Total	100	100

*The white adoptees are not included because the N's are too small; six children know their birth parents.

Seventy-eight percent of the parents said that there was no information that they did not or would not reveal to their children. Those who would withhold or have withheld information did so because the child was born out of wedlock, the mother was in prison, or siblings were born to the same mother.

PARENTS' ADVICE ABOUT TRANSRACIAL ADOPTION

In the first and third surveys we ended the formal interview by asking the parent:

> If a family in this community like your own, in terms of religious background, income, and education, asked you to advise them about whether they ought to adopt a nonwhite child, what specifically would you advise them to do?

In the first survey, save for 7 percent who answered that as a matter of principle they would not advise anyone on such an important personal decision, all but 3 percent said that they would urge the family to go ahead and adopt. Forty percent warned that the family should be very clear in their own minds that they are not making their decision because of their belief in "some social cause," "civil rights," "racial equality," or similar ideal. The parents' decision must be based, they emphasized, on how much they wanted a child and on their belief that they could offer the child a good home. Slogans, causes, and political ideology should have no place in their decision. Most of the parents mentioned that bad motives were "proving you are liberal," "wanting to do something noble," "taking a stand against the population explosion." The good motives were the "selfish ones," including wanting a child very badly.

Only one family said flatly: "We would not help any white family adopt a black child. We feel now that if a black child can find a black home this is ideal. If it were us today, knowing what we know, we would not do it."

Twelve years later, in 1984, 8 percent would not advise anyone as a matter of principle. Six percent would advise against TRA, and 1 percent were not sure what advice they would offer. The most negative reaction we heard was:

> We would urge couples not to have anything to do with TRA. We know several close friends who have adopted non-white children and in none of the cases has it worked out. The TRAs have left home and gone to live in a black community. We are glad we did it, but would not recommend it.

Eighty-six percent of the parents would urge transracial adoptions. One-third of them warned, as did 40 percent in 1972, that the family should have their motives and values straight, by which they meant that people should not adopt transracially because they think it is a "political cause." "Do not do it as part of a crusade," a mother warned. "Examine your motives," said many of the parents repeatedly. "Be sure of your own expectations and feelings about why you are doing this. Be open and committed to children. Do not adopt because you are trying to prove a point." "If they have to ask, they may be in trouble," was another reaction.

Forty-seven percent advised: "Adopt if you love and want children. Be sure you have a commitment to adoption." Or: "If a family really wants to do it, they should. It has been a good decision for us. Not without problems, but no child is." "They should decide whether they want a child, not a non-white child." "Pray about it. Keep your motives straight. Don't do it to wave a banner, but because you need a child to love." "Make sure you are not doing it out of white liberal guilt. It is not a status symbol, it is a commitment for a very long time."

But among those parents, about 25 percent warned that families have to be prepared to handle "the race issue" and specifically the "TRA" issue. A family who said that they had serious reservations about adoption per se emphasized that "a child has to be young enough for bonding."

Another family made some specific recommendations. The parents advised:

> Learn as much about the natural heritage of the child you are thinking about adopting as possible. Be prepared for problems different from those of biological birth kids. Take a hard look at realities, not just the liberal romantic aspects of adoption. Don't go into a transracial adoption naively or romantically. Transracial adoption at the time we did it was popular. Now, some families are having problems with their children. All things considered, though, we'd do it again.

Several other families stressed the importance of learning about the racial heritage of the child and of being prepared to teach adopted children about their heritage. "An adoptive couple should agree ahead of time how to handle the race issue." Another family said, "A couple should strive to make themselves aware of the *real* racial attitudes of their family, friends and community, because these attitudes will affect them, as well as their non-white adopted child."

Twelve years later, we find 86, rather than 90, percent of the families surveyed still willing to advise others like themselves to go ahead and adopt transracially. Stung as they were by the attacks of the black social workers and other groups, and tarnished as many have been by the experience of parenting, they still believe that what they did was right and good for their children.

NOTES

1. We asked for evaluations among all of the children in the families; but the combinations reported above are the ones in which the frequencies are worth reporting.

2. Ruth G. McRoy and Louis A. Zurcher, *Transracial and Inracial Adoptees* (Springfield, Ill.: Charles C. Thomas, 1983).

3. Ibid., p. 130.

4. Ibid., p. 131.

5. Ibid., p. 132.

6. Rita J. Simon and Howard Altstein, *Transracial Adoption: A Follow-up* (Lexington, Mass.: Lexington Books, 1981), p. 120.

5

The Children's Account

We interviewed 218 out of the 394 children in 96 families. Almost all of those whom we did not interview were older children who were no longer living in the parental home.[1] Fourteen children in 6 families were not interviewed because the parents objected, and 1 child was not interviewed because she did not want to participate. Those 6 families are described separately in Chapter 7. Among the 90 families in which at least 1 child was interviewed, 56 had one transracial adoptee at home, 23 families had two, 5 families had three, and 6 families had no TRAs at home.

Of the 218 children interviewed, 111 were transracially adopted, 91 were born to the families, and 16 were adopted but are white. Among the TRAs, 89 of the 111 are "black"[2] The breakdown by sex and age is shown below.

	TRA	Born	White Adoptee
Males	61	48	4
Females	50	43	12
Median Age	14.9	16.8	16.9

The TRAs are most likely to be the youngest children still at home, 81 percent of them compared to 17 and 1 percent of the children born into the family and the white adoptees, respectively.

All but 4 of the TRAs were still in school at the time of the study; 15 of the children born to the families and 4 of the other adoptees were no longer in school. Table 5.1 shows the breakdown by years, of those in school.

Among the children at the precollege level, 83 percent of the TRAs, 82 percent of those born into the family, and 80 percent of the white adoptees were attending public institutions. At the college level as well, most of the children were attending public universities, with no differences by adopted status.

Table 5.1: Year in School by Race and Adoptive Status

Year in School	TRA	Born	White/Adoptee
		(in percent)	
Less than 7th grade	3	--	--
7 - 8 grade	32	15	8
9 - 12 grade	58	55	75
13 - 16 grade	7	29	17
More than 16th grade	--	1	--
Total	100	100	100

The racial composition of the schools that the children attended were described by them as follows:

Racial Composition of Schools (in percent)

100–76 percent white	58
75–51 percent white	22
50 percent white	10
Less than 50 percent white	10

There was no greater likelihood of the TRAs attending schools that had a smaller percentage of white students than for the other respondents.

SCHOOL PERFORMANCE AND FUTURE EDUCATIONAL PLANS

The table below reports the average grades, according to the adolescents, that they received in school at the end of the last school year. Note that they match closely those reported by their parents.

	Mean Grade Last Year*
TRA	2.5
(Blacks)	2.4
Born	2.0
White/Adopted	2.0

*We converted an A to a score of 1, B to a 2, C to a 3, D to a 4, F to a 5.

The children seem to exhibit no tendency to "upgrade" their performance.

The plans of the TRAs and the children born into the families who are still in high school or junior high are quite similar; 75 percent of the TRAs said that they plan to go on to college or university, and 13 percent plan to attend some other type of school (trade, design, etc.). The others either plan to work or do not have a clear idea of what they want to do after high school. Given that the median age of the children in this category is not quite 15, it is not unusual that 12 percent claim that they have not decided what they will do three or four years hence.

Among the children born into the families, 94 percent expect to pursue college or university education and 4 percent plan to attend some type of trade school. Of the ten white adoptees who were still at the precollege level, one expects to travel, one expects to work, two have not decided, and the others plan to go on to college or university.

There was a large and varied range of occupations that respondents said they expected to go into when they completed their schooling. The most frequently cited areas of interest were law, business, teaching, and computers, although each of the four categories was mentioned by only 10 percent or less of the respondents. Adopted status made no difference in any of the choices.

The bases for their choices were "interests" and "skill," followed by "aptitude," "enjoyment," "wanting to help people," and "like children." Only 3 percent said that they were interested in a particular occupation or profession because they could make a lot of money in that field.

Parents or teachers did not seem to be an important consideration in making future plans; 6 percent of the respondents mentioned them as having significant influence. But 83 percent said that they thought their parents agreed with or supported their interests and preferences. When we asked the adolescents whether they thought their parents supported or agreed with their brothers' and sisters' choices, the TRAs, more than the children born into the families, said they believed that their parents approved of their siblings' choices (70 percent for the brothers and sisters). Among the children born into the families, 60 percent thought their parents approved of their transracially adopted brothers' plans, and 50 percent that their parents approved of the transracially adopted sisters' plans. However, 22 percent also said that they did not know their parents reactions, because their brothers or sisters had not expressed clear preferences about their future plans.

INTERESTS AND FRIENDSHIPS

Early in the interviews we asked the adolescents a series of questions about their interests, the kinds of activities in which they thought they excelled, special qualities that they attributed to themselves, the clubs they belonged to, and their friends.

For all three categories of adolescents, sports was the favorite activity named most often by 61 percent of the TRAs, 44 percent of the children born to the family, and 38 percent of the other adoptees. Music, reading, and crafts were some of the other activities named but never by more than 15 percent of any category of adolescents. Not surprisingly, of all activities, respondents thought that they were particularly good at sports (64 percent of the TRAs, 34 percent of the children born to the families, and 38 percent of the other adoptees).

We asked, "Are there some qualities about you that you think are special?" Table 5.2 shows the responses among the three categories. Most of the respondents answered that they did have special qualities, the majority focusing on relational and personality characteristics rather than on talents or skills, though the TRAs emphasized the former qualities to a somewhat lesser extent than did the other adolescents. The fact that the TRAs are on the average two years younger than the children in the other categories could account for the weaker emphasis on personality and interpersonal qualities.

Most of the respondents claimed not to belong to any clubs either at school or outside of school. The largest group who did were the TRAs, 31 percent of whom belonged to sports clubs. We also asked specifically about membership in clubs or organizations that represent an ethnic or racial type; 89 percent of the TRAs reported no affiliation, as did 92 and 94 percent of the other adolescents.

Table 5.2: Qualities Which Respondents Think Are Special by Race and Adoptive Status

| Qualities | Categories of Children | | |
	TRA	Born	White/ Adoptee
	(in percent)		
None	19.8	11.0	--
I am a good friend	21.6	24.2	31.3
People trust me, like to talk with me, think of me as a caring person	19.8	35.2	31.3
Physical skills	9.0	2.2	--
Special talent, other skills	12.6	5.5	--
Being adopted	2.7	--	6.3
Other	14.5	21.9	31.1
Total	100	100	100

Close friendships followed same sex lines, as is usually the case among all age groups in the United States. Thus, 88 percent of the TRAs chose same sex persons as their good friends, as did 84 percent of the adolescents in the other categories. But friendships within and across racial lines revealed different patterns among the three categories. The preferences are shown in Table 5.3.

The percentages in Table 5.3 show that black TRAs are almost as likely to choose white friends as are children in any of the other categories. The black children show a slightly greater tendency to select blacks as friends than do the white children or the TRAs of American Indian or Korean backgrounds. The opportunities for selecting black rather than white children as friends are obviously much smaller for all categories of children given the distribution of blacks in the communities in which the respondents live.

A 15-year-old black girl (of mixed parentage) commented: ''I hung around white kids until 6th grade; after that I made black friends because everyone was saying I was white when I knew I wasn't. I also kept my white friends.''

A 20-year-old respondent who described herself as ''black and white,'' and who was homecoming queen in her high school, described a series of incidents with blacks in high school who ''hassled'' her when she insisted that

Table 5.3: Friendship Choices by Race and Adoptive Status

Friend	TRA (Black)	TRA (Other)	Born	White/ Adoptee
		Category of Children		
		(in percent)		
		Friend #1		
White	73.2	76.0	88.6	68.8
Black	14.6	4.0	5.7	12.5
Other	6.7	4.0	3.4	12.5
No Answer	5.5	16.0	2.3	6.2
		Friend #2		
White	70.8	72.0	79.5	81.3
Black	19.1	12.0	10.2	6.3
Other	4.5	--	5.7	--
No Answer	5.6	16.0	4.6	12.4
		Friend #3		
White	61.8	56.0	71.6	81.3
Black	25.8	12.0	8.0	--
Other	3.4	--	8.0	--
No answer	9.0	32.0	12.4	18.7

she was both black and white. But she also described one event in which a group of black girls whom she had feared came over to her and told her that they were glad she was homecoming queen because they felt that she was representing them. On a different occasion one of the black girls at school asked her:

> Are you ashamed to be black?
> I said no. Then she asked why I didn't have any black friends and I said I'd be anyone's friend, I didn't care what they are; but I also explained that I was adopted into a white family; they didn't know that. The girls used to think I was acting white. If they said anything to me face to face I'd explain why I talked without slang and my family situation and my neighbors.

On the other hand, one 14-year-old black said, "I feel like a black person. I talk more to my black friend because he knows what I am talking about."

A young woman born into her family explained that she has had hassles with people whom she considered to be her friends because she had a black sister and because she dated black men. "Some of the people I thought were my friends have proven to have prejudiced attitudes."

About half of the respondents in each category said that they met their friends in the schools they attended. The neighborhood was named as the next most likely place.

In addition to querying the adolescents about their friends, we also asked them about whom they date and the parental reactions (their own parents and those of the dates) to the dating. Fifty-three percent of the TRAs said that they date (although 8 percent do so only in groups), as do 62 percent of the adolescents born into the families (10 percent only in groups) and 60 percent of the white adoptees (12 percent only in groups). The smaller percentage among the TRAs is probably explained by the fact that on the average they are two years younger than the children born into the families. The percentages among the white adoptees may not be meaningful because the frequencies on which they are based are so small. The racial characteristics among those who date are described in Table 5.4.

The TRAS are more likely to choose blacks as dates than as "good friends"; 38 percent said that they date blacks (though not exclusively), compared to 20 percent or so who named a black as their third closest friend. Sixteen percent of the born and 14 percent of the adopted white respondents also report that they date blacks, which, while lower than the cross-race dating reported by the TRAs, is nevertheless higher than what one is likely to find among a group of white adolescents in comparable communities.

Most of the respondents report that they have encountered no problems with either their own parents or those of their dates about their choice of date.

Table 5.4: Dating Choices by Race and Adoptive Status

Race of Dates	Categories of Children		
	TRA	Born	White/Adoptee
	(in percent)		
Whites exclusively	60	78	86
Blacks exclusively	11	6	--
Blacks and whites	27	10	14
Whites and ethnics	2	6	--
Total	100	100	100

But 29 percent of the TRAs said that they have encountered difficulties, twice as often from the parents of the date than from their own. Nineteen percent of the white adolescents also reported difficulties, and again primarily (70 percent of the time) from the parents of the person whom they were dating.

At the end of the interview, a transracially adopted black girl offered this observation: "I think it is a good idea for people to intermarry because then, someday, everyone will be the same color."

Another 17-year-old black adolescent complained: "When I'm with my white girl friends and we run into a group of guys, a lot of the guys are kind of prejudiced. No one asked me to the prom."

RACE AND FAMILY

Having focused thus far on the respondents' accounts of their schooling, activities, interests, and friendships, we shift now to the adolescents' perception of their families and their place in the family. We asked all of them:

In what ways is your family similar or different than your friends' families?

Most of the adolescents saw their family as similar to those of their friends in income level and socioeconomic status. That dimension was mentioned more often than any other by the TRAs and the children born into the families. Those characteristics were followed by the quality of the relationships, the families' values, and the number of children. The differences which the adolescents saw between their own family and the families of friends were in .

their decision not to adopt transracially (the difference cited most often by all three categories of respondents), the greater or lesser freedom parents allowed their children (there were as many respondents who said "more freedom" as there were respondents who said "less freedom"), the quality of family relationships, and the number of children. What we found most interesting about the comparisons between friends and respondents' families is the lack of difference in the perceptions of TRAs and the children born into the families concerning both the similarities and the differences among their own and their friends' families.

There were some issues that could only be discussed with the transracial adoptees. For example, we asked them:

 Can you tell me how it feels being (black, Korea, etc.) in a white family? Does it give you any problems or is it all straightforward?

Seventy-one percent of the TRAs answered that it gave them "no problems." They did not think about it; it was something that by this time they took for granted. Most others thought it embarrassing when they had to introduce their parents to new friends, or when they were in public and everyone with them was white.

One 16-year-old black adoptee said that she is embarrassed by her "white parents" in front of her black friends.

> My friends tease me when my parents come to school for conferences. They say, "Oh, my God, is that your mother? Ha, ha, your mother didn't want you." They also say I'm not as good as they are because my Mom and Dad are white. They said I don't act like a black person. It hurts me and makes me feel sad.

A 17-year-old black girl who described herself as "basically white inside" commented:

> Just being black in a white family is special—it draws a lot of attention to me, not all good. I feel more comfortable with whites; I'm uncomfortable around blacks. I don't act the same as they do or talke the way they do. I don't like the same music or activities.

Another 19-year-old black said, "When I was eight or nine years old I did not want to show my parents to my friends."

The TRAs were also asked:

Have there been times you wished you were of the same racial background as your parents?

Sixty percent of the respondents answered that "there has never been such a time." Among those who said that there have been such times, no one reason was given by more than 4 percent of the respondents. Such explanations were offered as: "It's upsetting when I'm at a family gathering and everyone is saying who looks like who and I wonder who I look like" and "When I'm with aunts, uncles, grandparents, and other members of the extended family." For example, a black daughter described a trip she took with her family to visit an aunt in South Dakota. She said: "There weren't any blacks there and I heard a lot of names. I've dealt with things like that before, but being the only black person there really made me feel like I wished I was white or any other color than black." Other reasons offered were: "At school, when I have to introduce my family to strangers"; "When shopping with my mother"; "I dislike having to explain to my friends why my parents are different."

All of the children were asked:

 Have there been times in your life when you wished you were another color?

Forty-three percent of the TRAs and 44 percent of the children born into the families said "never." Specifically, the times mentioned by both groups were at school and playing sports. It is interesting, and consistent with our observations about the TRAs' sense of belonging to their family, that they were no more likely to wish they belonged to "another" race than were their white siblings. One 20-year-old son born into his family who has one black brother said, "I'd like to be a chameleon so I could be the color that was most useful at the time."

A 16-year-old black girl commented at the end of the interview: "I really don't see my family as a white family. Each of us is color blind. Each person has his or her own personality." In another family, a child born into the family said about his black brother, "I don't look on him as a person of a different race. I look at him as a brother." A 14-year-old black girl commented, "Race doesn't matter; love is what is important."

One of the TRAs who expressed herself most vehemently and most negatively about her racial identity was an 18-year-old American Indian girl. She said: "It bothers me that I'm Indian. People don't look up to Indians. The whites always fought the Indians and the Indians got beat. We aren't looked up to. There is nothing special about being Indian." "Later on, when talking about her plans for the future, she said:

I'm not going to live on an Indian reservation and I'm not going to live in Minneapolis where all the blacks are. I don't like being with Indians and I don't want to be associated with blacks. They all stick together. You don't try to mix with them; they'd beat you up. Josh [her black brother] and I were beaten up five years ago by blacks. I want to live in a white community. I'm going to college and I plan to live in a dormitory. After college I'd like my kids to grow up in a white community.

A 20-year-old Korean who was adopted when he was ten years old reported:

When I was in Korea I wished I was a full Korean. I took more abuse over there than blacks receive here. I used to get into fights every day because of my American background. When I was the number one student in third grade, the school would not give me my award in public, the way they do for all the number one students in a class because they said "You are an American." The book they gave me said Number One in it, but there was no publicity about it.

The transracial adoptees were asked to remember if they experienced incidents in which "people were nasty or unpleasant about your racial background." Thirty-nine percent of the respondents said that they never experienced such an incident. The most frequently cited event among those who did was name calling in school (46 percent). Twenty-six percent cited insulting remarks made to them on the street or in a public place. The remaining 28 percent cited incidents such as when friends told jokes insulting to blacks in front of them, challenges to fight because of their color, and insulting remarks by teachers. But no more than 5 percent of the TRAs mentioned any one specific incident. Of those who described a certain event, half of them said that it occurred over two years ago. Sixty-three percent said that they told their parents about it. According to the respondents, most of the parents comforted them but "played down the incident" and did not take any action. Over half of the respondents also said that they did or said nothing to the perpetrator of the act.

The transracially adopted children were less likely to report that they and their parents "discuss race, racial differences, racial attitudes, and/or racial discrimination," as shown in the responses below.

Percent Reporting Race Discussed

TRAs	54.0
White/Born	79.3
White/Adopted	75.0

But there are no differences among the three categories of respondents to the following question:

When you sit back and think about how the world is organized, do you think in tems of racial categories; e.g., there are black, white, yellow, etc., people?

Percent Answering "Yes"

TRAs	22
White/Born	22
White/Adopted	23

One direct way to find out how important "race" is to the respondent's identity was to ask:

Imagine someone is meeting you at a train station who has never seen you before. How would you describe what you look like?

We divided the adolescents by their adopted status and by sex, because on this matter especially, we thought boys and girls might differ. The results are shown in Table 5.5.

Clearly, sex is not important; but race is. The white children (those born and adopted) are much less likely to mention the fact that they are white than are the transracial adoptees, of whom about 50 percent mention race as an identifying characteristic.

In the McRoy-Zurcher study, the authors assessed racial identity by a content analysis of the responses of 30 transracial and 30 black inracial adoptees' self-descriptions to the "Twenty Statements Test."[3] In the Twenty Statements Test, respondents are given the opportunity to answer the ques-

Table 5.5: Mentions of Race and Sex in Self-Descriptions by Race and Adoptive Status

Characteristics Mentioned	TRA Male	TRA Female	White/Born Male	White/Born Female	White/Adoptee Male*	White/Adoptee Female
			(in percent)			
Race	46.7	54.0	6.3	2.3	--	8.3
Sex	--	--	--	2.3	--	8.3
Race and Sex	3.3	4.0	6.3	2.3	--	--
Neither	46.7	40.0	85.4	88.4	--	75.0
Other/No answer	3.3	2.0	2.0	4.6	--	8.3
Total	100	100	100	100	--	100

*Frequencies are too small: N=4.

tion "Who Am I" 20 times. The results reported by McRoy and Zurcher are consistent with ours, insofar as they also found that the transracial adoptees were more likely than the inracial adoptees to refer to race in their self-descriptions. Twenty-seven percent of the inracial adoptees did so as opposed to 56 percent of the transracial adoptees.[4]

In our study, the differences were 52 percent for the TRAs (combining the male and female responses) as opposed to 8 percent for both the white born and white adoptees. This is lower than the percentage for black inracial adoptees in the McRoy-Zurcher study but demonstrates the greater salience of race among minority group respondents.

We also asked:

Which of the following statements fit how you really feel:
(a) I am proud to be (select one): black, brown Indian, Korean, white, other. Or,
(b) I do not mind what color I am. Or,
(c) I would prefer to be _____.

Sixty-six percent of the black TRAs answered that they are proud to be black or brown, 6 percent said that they are proud to be of "mixed background," 17 percent said that they did not mind what color they are, and 11 percent said that they would prefer to be white. Among the 22 Korean, native American, Vietnamese, and other TRAs, 82 percent said that they are proud to be whatever their racial heritage is, 9 percent said that they did not mind what color they are, and 9 percent said that they would prefer to be white.

Among the respondents born into the families, 84 percent said that they are proud to be white, 9 percent said that they do not mind what color they are, and 7 percent told us that they would prefer to be black, Spanish American, native American, or "different than I am." Seventy-five percent of the white adoptees said that they are proud to be white, 19 percent said, "I don't mind what color I am," and 6 percent said that they would prefer to be black.

McRoy and Zurcher reported that when the adoptees were asked to indicate whether they perceived themselves to be black, white, or mixed,

> seventeen (56%) of the TRAs referred to their racial background as being either mixed, part white, black-white, human or American; nine (30%) referred to themselves as black; three (10%) as white; and 1 responded Mexican. Inracial adoptees typically referred to themselves as black.[5]

FAMILY INTEGRATION AND COMMITMENT

When we first began this project in 1972, we did not focus on the children's sense of belonging to their adopted families. We did not foresee that questions of family integration, loyalty, and commitment would be crucial. In 1979, we were unable to interview the children. But in our most recent survey, we included items that probed how integrated into the family the adopted children felt themselves to be, and how committed both the adoptees and their parents are to their relationship. The most consistent and perhaps the most important finding emerging from this latest survey is the sense of belonging felt by the TRAs to their adopted families—the mothers and fathers are their parents, and the brothers and sisters, their siblings; they are not viewed as substitutes or proxies for "real" parents or "real" family. Even though the adoptees "look" different from their parents and siblings, they believe and feel themselves to be part of their adopted family.

Indeed, on every measure we included in this study, the TRAs responded consistently and strongly that they belonged to and felt a part of their family, and expected to continue to be family members in good standing when they left the parental home and organized their own lives. The TRAs were not "doing time" in their adopted homes; they plainly viewed the familial bonds as permanent and powerful.

The most direct evidence we have for these observations is the TRAs responses on (a) the Family Integration Scale; (b) questions asking: "To whom would you go when you feel (happy, sad, etc.); and (c) expectations about future closeness to parents and siblings.

We report first the responses to the Family Integration Scale. This scale was adopted from the latest survey of the British Adoption Project (BAP) by Owen Gill and Barbara Jackson, which they conducted in 1980–81.[6] The study included 44 families, 36 of whom had adopted transracially and 8 in which at least one parent was black. The data referred to from the Gill and Jackson study are based on the 36 TRA families. The distribution to each of the items by the four categories of respondents is described in Table 5.6.

Table 5.6: Family Integration Scale by Race and Adoptive Status

Family Integration Items	Categories of Children			
	TRA	Black	Born	White/ Adoptee
	(in percent)			
I enjoy family life:				
Strongly agree	40.4	40.4	46.6	37.5
Agree	53.7	51.7	50.0	50.0
Disagree	2.7	3.4	3.4	12.5
Strongly disagree	2.7	3.4	---	---
No answer	.5	1.1	---	---
I would like to leave home as soon as possible when I'm able to:				
Strongly disagree	10.0	9.0	14.8	18.8
Disagree	48.2	47.2	47.7	31.1

(continued)

Table 5.6: continued

Family Integration Items	TRA	Categories of Children		White/ Adoptee
		Black	Born	
		(in percent)		
Agree	34.2	37.1	29.5	31.3
Strongly agree	6.1	5.6	8.0	18.8
No answer	1.5	1.1	---	---
People in our family trust one another:				
Strongly agree	27.6	29.2	27.3	25.0
Agree	51.7	48.3	55.7	56.3
Disagree	19.7	20.2	17.0	18.7
Strongly disagree	.5	1.1	---	---
No answer	.5	1.2	---	---
Most families are happier than ours:				
Strongly disagree	23.2	25.8	31.8	18.8
Disagree	69.3	66.3	63.6	68.8
Agree	4.4	4.5	4.5	12.4
Strongly agree	2.6	2.2	---	---
No answer	.5	1.1	.1	---
I am treated in the same way as my brother and sister:				
Strongly agree	30.3	32.6	26.2	6.8
Agree	49.1	49.4	50.0	56.3
Disagree	13.1	12.4	22.7	18.1
Strongly disagree	7.0	4.5	1.1	18.8
No answer	.5	1.1	---	---
Most children are closer to their parents than I am:				
Strongly disagree	24.6	27.0	29.5	31.3
Disagree	53.5	53.9	54.5	31.3
Agree	16.2	14.6	14.8	31.3
Strongly agree	5.2	3.4	1.2	6.1
No answer	.5	1.1	---	---
If I'm in trouble, I know my parents will stick by me:				
Strongly agree	37.5	37.1	45.5	37.5
Agree	56.1	56.2	48.9	56.3
Disagree	5.4	5.6	5.6	6.2
Strongly disagree	.5	---	---	---
No answer	.5	1.1	---	---
My parents know what I am really like as a person:				
Strongly agree	20.2	22.5	20.4	12.5
Agree	62.3	60.7	68.2	62.5
Disagree	14.4	12.4	9.1	18.8
Strongly disagree	2.6	3.4	2.3	6.2
No answer	.5	1.1	---	---

We also computed mean and median scores for the four categories of respondents. The possible range was from 32 to 8: the lower the score, the higher the sense of family integration.

	N	Median	Mean	Standard Deviation
TRA	22	15.4	15.4	3.66
Black	89	15.3	15.2	4.27
Born	88	14.7	15.4	3.17
White/Adopted	16	15.5	16.7	4.00

The summary statistics as well as the percentages for each item shown in Table 5.6 fail to reveal any differences among the four categories of respondents. The TRAs perceive themselves as having the same type of relationship with their family as the other children.

In reporting the results of their study, Gill and Jackson said:

> The responses to these statements appear to show a general picture of family integration of these children with only a small number of children obtaining relatively low scores. There does, however, appear to be a difference between boys and girls on some of these questions. The four children showing the lowest family integration scores are all boys.[7]

We compared our TRAs and children born into the families by sex and also compared both groups against the Gill and Jackson respondents.[8] (See Table 5.7) On six of the eight items, there are greater differences between the boys and girls in the Gill and Jackson study than there are among our respondents. On the whole, in our study there are no strong differences between the transracially adopted boys and girls (save that the boys' percentages are consistently higher), and between the boys and girls born into the families.

The next set of items asked, "Who knows best what you are really like as a person and to whom would you go if..."

1. Of all the people in the family and outside, who knows best what you are really like as a person?

	Percent Responded Family Member*
TRA	54.2
Born	59.4
White adoptees	43.9

*For the TRAs and children born into the family, the responses include 2.7 and 3.3 percent, respectively, who answered "a grandparent."

2. If you were really happy about something that has gone right for you, which person inside or outside the family would you want to be the first to know?

	Percent Responded Family Member
TRA	66.6
Born	67.3
White adoptees	56.4

3. If you were really worried about something personal, who would you go to to talk about it?

	Percent Responded Family Member
TRA	46.8
Born	45.1
White adoptees	25.1

4. If you were wrongly accused of stealing something from a local shop, who would you go to to sort things out?

	Percent Responded Family Member
TRA	60.3
Born	68.2
White adoptees	31.0

The responses of the TRAs and the children born into the families are almost identical, while the white adoptees are much less likely to turn to a family member. (Remember that on the average the white adoptees are two and a half years older than the TRAs, but the same age as the children born into the families.)

The third measure of the strength of familial ties exhibited by the adolescents is shown in their responses to the following question:

Looking ahead to a time when you will not be living in your parents' house, do you expect that you will feel close to them (e.g., discuss things that are bothering you or that you consider important)?

We divided the respondents by sex as well as adopted status because of the popular belief that daughters are likely to feel closer to their parents than sons. Our results showed that there are no real differences by sex or adopted status.

Future Closeness to Parents

	TRA	Born
	Mean Scores*	
Males	2.2	2.1
Females	2.5	2.2

*1 = very close; 2 = close; 3 = fairly close; 4 = not at all close.

We also asked:

After you and your (brother and/or sister) have moved out of your parents' house, do you expect that you will be close to one another (e.g., talk on the phone a lot, spend time with each other, discuss things that are important to each of you)?

We computed means for older and younger siblings of the same and opposite sex. As in the findings reported for the parents, there are no real differences by sex or adopted status.

Table 5.7: Family Integration Scale by Adopted Status and Sex

Family Integration Items	TRAs M	F	Born M	F	Gill/Jackson M	F
	(in percent)					
Enjoy family life % Agree*	96.8	90.0	98.0	95.4	71.0	90.0
Would leave home % Disagree	62.3	52.0	58.4	69.8	57.0	57.0
Trust one another % Agree	78.7	78.0	85.4	81.4	57.0	73.0
Happier than ours % Disagree	96.8	88.0	93.8	97.7	57.0	95.0
Treated same as siblings % Agree	83.6	70.0	81.2	71.1	43.0	100
Closer to parents % Disagree	80.3	74.0	83.3	86.0	43.0	82.0
Stick by me % Agree	95.1	90.0	95.8	93.0	71.0	86.0
Know me % Agree	86.9	76.0	89.6	88.4	71.0	82.0

* The Strongly Agree and Agree responses were combined to match the Gill and Jackson categories.

Future Closeness to Siblings

	TRA	Born
Older Siblings of Same Sex		
Males	2.6	2.5
Females	2.6	2.3
Older Siblings of Opposite Sex		
Males	2.6	2.3
Females	2.6	2.7
Younger Siblings of Same Sex		
Males	2.4	2.4
Females	2.5	2.1
Younger Siblings of Opposite Sex		
Males	2.5	2.6
Females	2.9	2.0

As expected, there was a significant positive correlation between the Family Integration Scores and the expected future closeness to parents and siblings among the three categories of respondents.

Family Integration Scores and Future Closeness to Parents

TRAs	Born
r = .37	r = .36
p = .000	p = .000

Family Integration Scores and Future Closeness to Siblings

TRAs	Born
r = .41	r = .33
p = .000	p = .01

Further evidence for our contention that the TRAs are as integrated into their families as the children who were born into them is the lack of differences we found in the responses to questions about the ties and feelings they have toward grandparents, aunts and uncles, and other members of their extended family. Among the TRAs, 82 percent have at least one grandparent still alive, and 71 percent said that they feel close to their grandparents. Among the children born into the family, 84 percent have grandparents who are still alive, and 53 percent feel close to them; and among the white adoptees, 87 percent have grandparents who are still alive, and 57 percent feel close to them. Forty-four percent of the TRAs, 50 percent of the children born into the families, and 38 percent of the white adoptees said that they visit or talk over the phone with their grandparents at least once a month. Essentially, the same pattern was repeated in response to questions about the adolescents' ties to their aunts and uncles. Thus, in their relations with extended family members, the transracial adoptees define themselves as having at least as close ties with their relatives as the children born into the families. The TRAs do not sense that they are outsiders or that they are not accepted.

SELF-ESTEEM

In a 1968 study conducted in Baltimore of 1,917 pupils in 26 schools, in grades ranging from 3 to 12, Morris Rosenberg and Roberta Simmons measured "self-esteem" among black and white respondents by asking the pupils to respond to the seven items listed below.

- I feel I have a number of good qualities.
- I feel I do not have much to be proud of.
- I take a positive attitude toward myself.
- On the whole, I am satisfied with myself.
- I wish I could have more respect for myself.
- At times I think I'm no good at all.
- I certainly feel useless at times.[9]

These seven items were lifted from an earlier study conducted in New York State by Rosenberg of high school juniors and seniors in which he measured self-esteem by including these three additional items.

- I am a person of worth, at least on an equal plane with others.
- All in all, I am inclined to feel that I am a failure.
- I am able to do things as well as most other people.[10]

Rosenberg and Simmons are careful to explain what they mean by self-esteem in the following paragraphs.

> The aspect of the self with which we are concerned in this study is one concisely described by Gardner Murphy as "the individual as known to the individual.". . . Thus, the individual's conscious beliefs, opinions, attitudes, values, and feelings about himself are encompassed in this definition.
>
> Our chief, though not exclusive, concern is the individual's positive or negative orientation toward this object, his favorable or unfavorable attitudes toward it, and the associated emotional reactions. . . When we characterize

a child as having high self-esteem [we mean] that he considers himself a person of worth. He has fundamental respect for himself, appreciating his own merits, even though he is aware of faults in himself which he hopes and expects to overcome. The person with high self-esteem does not necessarily consider himself better than most others, but neither does he consider himself worse. Low self-esteem means that the individual lacks respect for himself, considers himself unworthy, inadequate or otherwise seriously deficient as a person.[11]

They reported the self-esteem scores for black and white children by age as shown in Table 5.8.

We see that in each age group a greater percentage of black children have high self-esteem than do white children. Rosenberg and Simmons comment on these results as follows: "These data thus clearly challenge the widespread assumption that black children are conspicuously low in self-esteem."[12]

When they compared the grades on report cards for the black and white children by self-esteem scores, they found that while grades made a difference, they made less of a difference for black than for white pupils. The pupils' socioeconomic status functioned in the same way as grades; namely, it bore upon the self-esteem of white children but had no effect on that of blacks.

After examining a great number of other factors that might influence self-esteem, Rosenberg and Simmons concluded that one factor provided an important, indeed crucial, explanation for why black children do not have lower self-esteem despite "the immense disprivileges" to which they are subject. That factor is the role of "significant others." Using a six-item scale that included how the respondents believe their friends, kids in their class, teachers, and mothers perceive them, Rosenberg and Simmons found a strong association between the respondents' self-esteem, on the one hand, and their belief that significant others hold positive attitudes toward them on the other. Table 5.9 describes that relationship.

Table 5.8:   Self-Esteem by Age and Race*

Self-Esteem	8-11 Black	White	12-14 Black	White	15-19 Black	White
	(Percent)					
Low	20	39	23	37	15	35
Medium	35	31	37	31	31	27
High	45	30	40	32	54	37
N=100 %	508	211	320	257	292	187

*From Morris Rosenberg and Roberta G. Simmons, Black and White Self-Esteem: The Urban School Child (Washington, D.C.: American Sociolgical Association, 1971), p. 5.

Table 5.9: Self-Esteem and Attitudes Attributed to Significant Others, by Race*

Self-Esteem	Blacks				Whites			
	Attitudes of significant others perceived as:							
	Favor-able			Un-favor-able	Favor-able			Un-favor-able
	1	2	3	4	1	2	3	4
				(in percent)				
Self-Esteem								
Low	4	13	26	38	38	32	41	61
Medium	26	36	38	39	19	28	36	28
High	70	51	36	23	43	40	23	12
N=100%	(50)	(409)	(252)	(69)	(21)	(286)	(116)	(33)

*From Rosenberg and Simmons, op. cit., p. 144.

They concluded:

> We thus see that significant others do play a most important role in the formation of the child's self-esteem—more important, indeed, than virtually any of the other factors we have considered. Furthermore, as we examine various measures of association, we find that the relationship between significant others' attitudes and self-esteem appears to be somewhat stronger among black than among white children. But with regard to the perceptions of significant others, we have seen, the black children are at no serious disadvantage. These are the influences which really count for the black children and which so effectively serve to protect their self-esteem.[13]

Since most of our respondents are adolescents in their junior and senior years of high school, we used the original ten-item Self-Esteem Scale to see if the black children in our study were likely to score higher or lower than the white children. As shown in Table 5.10, we also separated out the white adoptees from the white adolescents who had been born into the families, and the other transracial adoptees from the larger group of black adoptees.

The highest possible score is 40 and the lowest 10. The lower the score, the higher the self-esteem. Only the scores of respondents who answered all ten items were included in computing the means and medians shown below.

Categories of Respondents	N	Median	Mean	Standard Deviation
Black	86	17.8	18.1	3.49
Other TRAs	17	18.0	18.3	3.66
Born	83	18.1	18.0	3.91
White/Adoptee	15	18.0	18.5	3.16

Table 5.10: Self-Esteem by Race and Adopted Status

Self-esteem item	TRA	Black	Born	White/Adopted
		(in percent)		
1. I take a positive attitude toward myself.				
Strongly agree	32.4	32.6	44.3	18.8
Agree	64.9	62.9	51.1	81.2
Disagree	2.7	3.4	4.5	--
Strongly disagree	--	--	--	--
No answer	--	1.1	1.1	--
2. I wish I could have more respect for myself.				
Strongly disagree	9.9	10.1	15.9	12.4
Disagree	55.9	60.7	47.8	43.8
Agree	29.7	24.7	31.8	43.8
Strongly agree	4.5	4.5	4.5	--
No answer	--	--	--	--
3. I am a person of worth, at least on an equal plane with others.				
Strongly agree	45.0	42.7	39.8	31.3
Agree	52.3	56.2	56.8	56.3
Disagree	2.7	1.1	3.4	12.4
Strongly disagree	--	--	--	--
No answer	--	--	--	--
4. I certainly feel useless at times.				
Strongly disagree	12.6	13.5	12.8	--
Disagree	36.0	33.7	31.5	37.5
Agree	43.2	43.8	48.9	56.3
Strongly agree	8.2	9.0	6.8	6.2
No answer	--	--	--	--
5. I feel I have a number of good qualities.				
Strongly agree	33.3	34.8	44.3	43.8
Agree	64.0	64.0	54.5	56.2
Disagree	2.7	1.2	1.2	--
Strongly disagree	--	--	--	--
No answer	--	--	--	--
6. All in all, I am inclined to feel that I am a failure.				
Strongly disagree	55.9	61.8	69.3	56.2
Disagree	40.5	36.0	27.3	43.8
Agree	2.6	2.2	3.4	--
Strongly agree	--	--	--	--
No answer	.9	--	--	--

Table 5.10: continued

Self-esteem item	TRA	Black	Born	White/ Adopted
7. I am able to do things as well as most other people.				
Strongly agree	36.9	38.2	29.5	31.3
Agree	59.5	59.6	68.2	56.3
Disagree	3.6	2.2	2.3	12.4
Strongly disagree	--	--	--	--
No answer	--	--	--	--
8. I feel I do not have much to be proud of.				
Strongly disagree	41.4	43.8	46.6	62.5
Disagree	54.1	53.9	46.6	31.3
Agree	3.6	2.3	6.8	6.2
Strongly agree	.9	--	--	--
9. On the whole, I am satisfied with myself.				
Strongly agree	29.7	30.4	35.3	37.5
Agree	64.9	67.4	59.1	62.5
Disagree	4.5	2.2	4.5	--
Strongly disagree	--	--	1.1	--
No answer	.9	--	--	--
10. At times I think I'm no good at all.				
Strongly disagree	23.5	23.6	23.9	25.0
Disagree	45.0	46.1	43.2	56.2
Agree	30.6	30.3	31.8	18.8
Strongly agree	--	--	--	--
No answer	.9	--	1.1	--

There are no meaningful differences among the four categories of adolescents on their overall self-esteem scores. Unlike the black and white respondents in the Rosenberg and Simmons study, the black adolescents in our study did not score higher on "self-esteem."

McRoy and Zurcher also reported self-esteem scores, which they measured by using the self-esteem component of the Tennessee Self-Concept Scale. High scorers on the self-esteem component of the Tennessee Scale like themselves and feel that they are persons of worth. Low scorers evaluate themselves negatively and doubt their worth as individuals. The mean for the scale's norming samples who are white, nonadopted individuals was 345.6. McRoy and Zurcher reported means of 348.9 for the TRAs and 348.7 for the inracial adoptees.[14] Thus, their data, as did ours, revealed no differences in self-esteem scores by race, nor did the adoptive status of the respondents affect their scores.[15]

We also correlated the self-esteem scores by grades in school and found a significant relationship only for the 22 nonblack TRAs. We also tested for the strength of the association between family integration and self-esteem by correlating the scores of each scale by the four categories of respondents. We found, as shown below, strong and positive relationships for three of the four categories. Only among the white adoptees was the relationship not significant.

Correlations Between "Family Integration" and "Self-Esteem"

Blacks	$r = .40$	$p = .000$
Other TRAs	$r = .24$	$p = .008$
Born	$r = .47$	$p = .000$
White/Adoptees	$r = .15$	$p = .29$

Thus, among the black and other nonwhite adoptees and among the children born into the family, those who had close ties also experienced high self-esteem.

THE FUTURE

Toward the end of the interview we asked all of the adolescents a series of questions about their future. The topics focused on choice of marriage partners, types of communities in which they planned to live, participation in ethnic organizations, and, for the adoptees, any interest or plans they might have to try to locate their birth parents.

On the items pertaining to the types of communities in which the respondents are likely to live when they are "on their own," and whether they are likely to join an ethnic association, the results showed a consistent pattern. The majority of the respondents in each category (the TRAs, the white adoptees, and the children born into the families) expect to live in mostly white or mixed neighborhoods, and they do not anticipate joining any ethnic organization. The distribution of responses is shown in Table 5.11.

There are several interesting features about the responses in Table 5.11. First, only 2 percent of the TRAs said that they plan to live in a mostly black neighborhood. Second, a higher percentage of TRAs, as opposed to children born into the families, plan to live in a mostly white neighborhood. Third, the large majority of white children born into the families, like their TRA siblings, plan to live in "mixed" racial neighborhoods. These findings are consistent with the other data that showed the desires of the TRAs to live their adult lives in an environment and culture similar to the one in which they were reared by their adopted parents. Their white siblings, on the other hand, do

Table 5.11: Type of Community Expect to Live In by Race and
Adoptive Status

Type of Community Likely to Live in On Their Own	Respondents by Adoptive Status		
	TRA	Born	White /Adoptee
	(in percent)		
Mostly white	26.6	10.3	50
Mixed (white and black)	63.8	76.5	50
Mostly black	2.2	--	--
Mostly other combination	--	2.9	--
Don't know	7.4	8.9	--
No answer	--	1.4	--
Total	100	100	100

not want to live in a white environment. They have been influenced by the presence of their nonwhite siblings and do not see themselves fitting into a traditional white world.

The distribution of responses to the next item, which concerns the likelihood of their participating in ethnic organizations, is shown in Table 5.12. In each category the large majority do not expect to participate in "ethnic organizations." Again, the pattern is similar among the three categories and, again, the TRAs do not expect to shift their adopted lifestyle to one that more closely matches their outward appearance.

Table 5.12: Expected Participation in Ethnic Organizations by
Race and Adoptive Status

Participation in Ethnic Organization	Respondent by Adoptive Status		
	TRA	Born	White/Adoptee
	(in percent)		
Yes, black organization	8.1	1.1	--
Yes, other ethnic organization	8.1	12.0	--
Maybe, probably not	14.4	7.7	12.5
Will not participate	48.6	49.5	68.8
Don't know/no answer	20.8	29.7	18.7
Total	100	100	100

The responses on the marriage question are somewhat more complicated. As shown by the distribution in Table 5.13, the TRAs are less likely to separate themselves from their ethnic heritage on this issue than they are on the other two.

And, as the responses show, the white adolescents are more committed than the TRAs to marrying someone of their own background. On the other hand, with one exception, none of the TRAs said that they expect to marry a white person, even though 27 percent expect to live in a mostly white community. The higher percentage of "don't knows" among the TRAs is probably also a function of the age spread among the three categories of respondents.

The responses to the three items about important aspects of their future behavior characterize quite accurately the TRAs' perception of their world as essentially pluralistic and multicolored, and that they expect to find a place in that world. Their white siblings share that view. They too perceive the world to be more pluralistic than do white adolescents who have not grown up in a special environment. McRoy and Zurcher's transracial adoptees seem to share a similar view. They report that "twenty-three (77%) expressed acceptance of and interest in interracial marriage."[16] But their black adoptees seemed more definite in their choice of a mate of the same race (90 percent

Table 5.13: Choice of Marriage Partners by Race and Adoptive Status

Racial Characteristics of Likely Mate	Respondents by Adoptive Status		
	TRA	Born	White/Adoptee
	(in percent)		
White	1.1	65.4	78.6
Black	23.3	1.3	---
Asian	3.3	---	---
Native American	7.7	6.4	7.1
Mixed	2.1	--	---
Don't know, but probably not someone of same racial background	23.3	5.1	---
Other	9.2	3.9	---
Don't know	30.0	17.9	14.3
Total	100	100	100

said that they expect to marry a black person) than did our white adoptees and white adolescents born into the family.

We shift now to another aspect of the respondents' future, one that affects only the adopted children. We asked them:

Would you like to be able to locate your birth parents?
Have you tried to locate them?

The distribution of responses looked like this:

Want to or Have Tried to Locate Birth Parents*

Yes, and have tried	22.5
Yes, but have not tried thus far	15.3
Not sure, maybe in future	25.2
No	37.0

*The responses are given only for the TRAs. The N's are too small for the white adoptees, six of whom know who their birth parents are.

Thirty-eight percent of the TRAs have already tried or have some interest in locating their birth parents. When we asked why, most answered: "Curiosity. I'd like to see what I'm going to look like when I'm older." A few said "to find out why they gave me up," or "because I'll feel incomplete until I do."

None of the respondents said that they were looking for their "real" parents, or that they hoped to be reunited with their birth parents or family. The adolescents were expressing a sense of incompleteness about their origins and a need for more information about their personal histories. They are not, we believe, declaring an ambivalence about their adopted parents or uncertainty about their feelings of belonging to their adoptive families. Indeed, all the issues discussed in this chapter confirm the adopted adolescents' commitment to their families and their involvement with their adoptive parents, siblings, and other relatives.

NOTES

1. There were 92 such children; 35 were not interviewed because they were too young (under 12 years of age); 34 were not interviewed because they were away at school and a suitable time could not be arranged after several attempts; or the parents were divorced and the children were living, temporarily or permanently, with the parent who had moved away.

2. Included in the "black" category are children of mixed "black and white" backgrounds.

3. Ruth G. McRoy and Louis A. Zurcher, *Transracial and Inracial Adoptees* (Springfield, Ill.: Charles C. Thomas, 1983).

4. Ibid., p. 128.

5. Ibid., p. 127.

6. Owen Gill and Barbara Jackson, *Adoption and Race* (New York: St. Martin's Press, 1983).

7. Ibid., p. 39.

8. Gill and Jackson combined their "strongly agree" and "agree," and "strongly disagree" and "disagree" categories. To make the comparisons useful, we did the same in Table 5.7. Having shown that there were no differences between the black and other TRAs, we combined them and compared only the difference by sex. Once the white adoptees are divided by sex, the Ns are too small to make any meaningful comparisons between the boys and girls, so we have not included the white adoptees' responses.

9. Morris Rosenberg and Roberta G. Simmons, *Black and White Self-Esteem; The Urban School Child*, Arnold M. and Caroline Rose Monograph Series (Washington, D.C.: American Sociological Association, 1971).

10. Morris Rosenberg, *Society and the Adolescent Self-Image* (Princeton, N.J.: Princeton University Press, 1965).

11. Rosenberg and Simmons, op. cit., p. 9. Rosenberg and Simmons used only the seven-item scale in their Baltimore study because they found in their pretest of "lower-class third-grade children" that "some could not understand all the words."

12. Ibid., p. 5.

13. Ibid., p. 144.

14. McRoy and Zurcher, op. cit., p. 118.

15. In the fall of 1984, Marlene Ross, a doctoral candidate in the School of Education at The American University, conducted a study of the educational needs of adoptive parents in the District of Columbia. In the course of her study she interviewed 29 white families who had adopted a white child and 9 black families who had adopted a black child. All of the adoptees in her study were adolescents between the ages of 13 and 18. One of the instruments she included in the interview schedule for the adolescents was the self-esteem scale. The means and medians for her white and black adoptees were 17.3 for the white adoptees and 17.1 for the black adoptees. As we discovered in our survey, Ross did not find that black adolescents had higher self-esteem than whites; rather, there were no differences by race among the two groups of adoptees. Our results also showed no difference by race and adoptive status.

16. McRoy and Zurcher, op. cit., p. 68.

6

How the Parents' and Children's Accounts Match Up

This chapter compares responses to questions that were asked of both the parents and the adolescents in their separate interviews. The topics concern the racial characteristics of friends and dates, grades in school, favorite activities, consensus or lack of it about the adolescent's future vis-a-vis schooling and work. It also compares the parents' and adolescents' perceptions of how close they will be to each other when the adolescent leaves the family home, as well as comparing their expectations about the racial characteristics of the community in which the adolescent is likely to live as an adult and the racial background of the adolescent's choice of a marriage partner. Responses on the adolescents' interests in finding their birth parents and the likelihood that they will try to do so are also compared.

We found in examining these issues that, on the whole, the parents' and adolescents' responses reflect considerable consensus and similarity of opinions. The parents' responses by and large indicate that they understand their children, and the adolescents' responses reflect views and lifestyles that are shared by their parents. Our overall impression of these families is supported by these responses—the families are an integrated unit; the adoption has bound them together and has developed and strengthened ties or commitments to each other that racial differences have neither weakened nor broken, nor are they likely to do so. As different as the children may look from their parents and siblings, they are an integral part of the family, and the assumption of independence because of adulthood is not likely to cause a breakup of the family unity. The children of the TRAs will be in every sense the grandchildren of these parents and the nieces and nephews of their brothers and sisters. Their physical departure and separation from the family will not disrupt or cut off family ties and commitments between the adopted children and their parents.

We compare first the adolescents' reports about the racial characteristics of their friends and the parents' reports about their children's friendships. Among the adolescents, we had shown that 74 percent of the TRAs, 89 percent of the children born into the families, and 69 percent of the white adoptees named a white person as their first close friend. In describing their oldest (who is still living at home) child's friends, the parents reported that 72 percent of the TRAs, 87 percent of the children born to them, and 77 percent of the white adoptees had only white friends. The second and third close friends described by the adolescents and the close friends reported by the parents for their second and third children produce the same pattern. Namely, the parents' perceptions about the racial characteristics of their children's friends matched quite closely the adolescents' own reports about their close friends.

There was also a close match between reports of whom the adolescents date and the parents' descriptions of their children's choice of dates. For example, 60 percent of the TRAs said that they date only whites, 78 percent of the adolescents born into the families report that they date only whites, and 86 percent of the white adoptees date only whites. In describing the racial characteristics of their children's dates, the parents state that among the TRAs, 72 percent date only whites, and among the children born to them 84 percent date only whites. (There are too few parents of white adoptees to be worth reporting.)

McRoy and Zurcher summarize their data on friendships and dates as follows:

> The transracial adoptees were more likely to have white friends and dates, and the inracial adoptees were more likely to have black friends and dates. Patterns of association due to the racial composition of the community and school was the key factor in determining the race of the adoptees' friends. . . . Most transracial adoptees stated that they would date either blacks or whites but tended to prefer to date members of the racial group with which they were most familiar in their social milieu.[1]

They reported that the percentage of TRAs who said that most of their school and community friends were white was 86 percent, and 83 percent indicated that their best friend was white. Among the inracial adoptees, only 10 percent said that the majority of their friends were white, and 6 percent reported that their best friends were white.

These responses generally coincide with those reported by the adolescents in our study. The large majority of the TRAs whom we interviewed have white friends, and a large majority of the white children (born and adopted) have same race friends, which means '''white.''

But the responses in our study about dating differ from those in McRoy and Zurcher's: our TRAs are more likely to date whites exclusively. While McRoy and Zurcher report that 71 percent of the TRAs in their survey stated "that either black or white dates were acceptable," only 23 percent said that they preferred to date whites, and only 6 percent revealed that they would date only blacks.[2] One explanation for the difference might be that more adolescents in the McRoy and Zurcher study sound as if they are describing hypothetical events rather than actual behavior. These TRAs believe that, in theory, dating persons of both races is preferable to limiting one's dates to either whites or blacks.

An examination of the responses by adolescents and parents concerning the former's favorite activities shows the same pattern. For both the parents and the three types of adolescents, sports is the favorite activity, as well as the activity, according to both parents and adolescents, at which the adolescents are particularly good.

Even on the matter of grades, where one might be more likely to expect discrepancies in reports between parents and children, the similarities are strong. The average grade reported by the TRAs last year was 2.5. For the parents describing the first, second, and third TRAs at home (or away at college), the average grades reported were 2.5, 2.6, and 2.7, respectively. The children born into the families reported an average grade last year of 2.0. The parents of such children reported 1.8, 1.8, and 2.1 for the first, second, and third child. Among the white adoptees, the average grade was 2.0. The parents reported 2.7 and 2.0 for the first and second white adoptees. These latter figures may not be reliable because there were less than 10 respondents involved.

Comparisons between parents' and children's accounts of the frequency with which they discussed "'racial issues'" revealed that more parents than TRA children reported such discussions. Concerning the children's responses, we noted that the TRAs were less likely to report that such discussions took place than were their white siblings; but the percentages reported by parents and white children were close (87 and 79 percent). Perhaps what is considered a discussion about "'race'" by persons in the majority is not so perceived by those who are often the target of such conversations.

We did find that parents and TRA children were in agreement about the frequency with which the TRAs experienced insults or were the targets of racial slurs. Sixty-one percent of the TRAs reported such incidents, as did 65 percent of the parents. An additional 7 percent of the parents thought that such incidents might have occurred without the children telling them about it. The parents and children also agreed about the nature of the incidents and their actual as well as likely impact. Almost always they involved name calling by other children, and they are not believed to have left a "'lasting'" impression or scar.

Shifting to the future, we compared parents' and adolescents' expectations about how close they would be to each other. Unfortunately, the scales on the two interview schedules were not the same. On the parents' questionnaire, the choices were (1) close, (2) fairly close, (3) fairly distant, and (4) distant. On the adolescents' questionnaire, the choices were (1) very close, (2) close, (3) fairly close, and (4) not at all close. In each category, the lower the score, the greater the closeness. Even though the scales are not identical, the findings nevertheless confirmed the lack of difference in the parents' expectations of closeness with the TRA, born, and white adopted children, and also supported the lack of difference among the children's expectations about how close they are likely to be with their parents. The ratings are shown below as mean scores.

Future Closeness Between Parents and Children

Parents' Ratings About Child*

TRAs			Born			White/Adopted		
1st	2nd	3rd	1st	2nd	3rd	1st	2nd	3rd
1.8	1.6	1.6	1.4	1.7	1.6	1.8	—	—

*1 = Close, 2 = Fairly close

Adolescents' Rating About Parents*

TRAs	Born	White/Adopted
2.3	2.2	2.3

*1 = Very close; 2 = Close

The results also show that even accounting for the differences in the scales, the adolescents expect to be closer to their parents than the parents expect to be to their children.

Comparisons between the parents' and adolescents' expectations about future closeness among siblings reveal a similar pattern. The adolescents expect to be closer to each other, regardless of race or adopted status, than the parents expect that their children will be, irrespective of race and adopted status. The means presented below compare the expectations of the parents regarding their children's closeness to each other against those of the children's expectations about how close they are likely to be with each other in the future.

Remembering that "2" signifies "fairly close" in the parents' scale, while "2" represents "close" in the children's scale, we see that the adolescents'

Parents' Ratings	Children's Ratings	
First Adopted and First Born 2.0*	Older Sibling of Same Sex	
	TRA 2.6*	Born 2.4
First Adopted and Second Born 2.0	Older Sibling of Opposite Sex	
	TRA 2.6	Born 2.5
Second Adopted and First Born 2.1	Younger Sibling of Same Sex	
	TRA 2.5	Born 2.3
Second Adopted and Second Born 1.8	Younger Sibling of Opposite Sex	
	TRA 2.7	Born 2.3
Among Adopted Children 2.0		
*1 = Close, 2 = Fairly close	*1 = Very close, 2 = Close	

expectations are still somewhat more positive than those of the parents concerning closeness among siblings.

Still focusing on the future, we compared parents' and adolescents' expectations about the racial characteristics of the latter's choices of marriage partners and the types of communities in which they would choose to live. We found most of the parents reluctant to speculate about those issues. Among those who were willing to make a prediction, twice as many thought that their black children would marry someone whose racial characteristics matched their own, and that their other nonwhite children (e.g., Koreans, native Americans) would be as likely to marry a white person as they would be to marry a member of their own community, because the opportunities for meeting others of similar racial background are much more limited. We did not ask the parents for their expectations about their birth children.

Among the adolescents, 30 percent of the TRAs said that they did not want to speculate about the racial characteristics of the person they were likely to marry, but among those who did, almost twice as many replied a black or a member of another ethnic community. Among the white adolescents willing to speculate (and 85 percent were willing to do so), about one in five expected to marry a nonwhite. On the issue of marriage partners, except for the greater reluctance of the parents to speculate about this issue, the projections of those parents who were willing to respond did not differ in any significant manner from the expectations of their adopted children.

Concerning their expectations about the racial characteristics of the community in which their TRAs are likely to live, among those willing to guess

(72 percent), half of the parents thought that they would live in the same type of community in which they had been reared, that is, primarily white middle and upper middle class. About one-quarter thought that they would live in a mixed racial community, and the remaining 12 percent believed that they would live in a black community. The TRAs were more likely than their parents to feel that they would live in racially mixed or nonwhite communities. Sixty-four percent expect to live in mixed communities, 2 percent in mostly black, and 27 percent in mostly white communities. The remaining 7 percent said that they did not know. Interestingly, only 10 percent of the white children expected to live in predominantly white communities such as the one in which they were reared.

We conclude from these responses that the experience of multiracial living seems to have been internalized by the children more successfully than the parents anticipated, as demonstrated by the responses of the white children who said that they would seek out mixed communities, and the 20 percent or so who would also marry across racial lines. But rather than view their responses as representing a separation from or rejection of their parents' values, the children's responses may be interpreted as having adapted to and accepted those values beyond the parents' expectations.

The last topic on which we compared the adolescents' and parents' responses was the delicate issue of birth parents—the adopted adolescent's desire to find them and the parents' willingness to cooperate. Forty-seven percent of the parents said that their TRA children have thus far shown no interest in learning about or learning *more* about their birth parents, or in locating them. Seven percent said that they had already given their children whatever information they had about their parents, and some were already in contact with them. The parents reported that the others expressed varying degrees of interest ranging from "'they have asked but have shown no desire to locate or contact them'' (29 percent) to discussing plans ''to try and find them'' (12 percent). The adolescents' responses were markedly similar. Thirty-seven percent said that they have no interest in locating their birth parents. Thirty-eight percent have tried to locate them or have expressed interest in locating their birth parents. Twenty-five percent told us that they had not yet tried to find their birth parents. They might do so later on, when they were adults.

Of all the issues discussed, the matter of birth parents is likely to be the most divisive and the one about which adoptees are least likely to be candid in their discussions with their adopted parents. It is also an issue about which the adopted parents are more likely to allow their wishes and hopes to cloud their perceptions of their children's behavior. Yet, even on this topic, the parents seem to be reading their children's interests and plans quite accurately. The majority of the children do not seem to be overcome with curiosity, desire, or need to find their birth parents.

NOTES

1. Ruth G. McRoy and Louis A. Zurcher, *Transracial and Inracial Adoptees* (Springfield, Ill.: Charles C. Thomas, 1983), pp. 81–82.

2. Ibid., p. 68.

7

Special Families: Problems, Disappointments, Conflicts

This chapter focuses on families who characterized their current relationships with each other as problematic and troublesome. It also provides updates on families who reported problems in 1979; and it reviews information from the two earlier phases of the study about the ten families who participated in the 1979 survey and refused to participate in the 1983–84 study. We also profile the six families in which the parents refused to allow their children to participate, but agreed to participate themselves.

In 1979, we allowed the parents to define what the major family problems were and to label themselves as families whose problems stemmed from the adoption. In this phase, because we interviewed the children, and because they are old enough to make evaluations, we have used the parents' and/or the children's definition of the situation as the basis for labeling a family as one that has problems.

FAMILIES WHO REFUSED TO BE INTERVIEWED

Seven of the families who refused to be interviewed were in the Minneapolis–St. Paul region. Two of these families were having problems when we interviewed them in 1979. In one family, the mother traced the problems to an accident that had occurred in 1971 when their transracially adopted six-year-old son was hit by an automobile. The accident left him physically impaired and brain damaged. In 1979 the mother reported: "There have been lots of problems since the accident. He's very irritable to his sisters. He is not doing well in school. He has problems making friends although he tries." During the interview, the mother complained that there were "too many studies being done about transracial adoption." She agreed reluctantly to participate in this one, but told us that she had refused most of the others. In 1984 she repeated her belief that there is an "inordinate amount of studies about transracial adoption"; she did not feel it necessary to defend her decision to adopt transracially and thought that it was an imposition on the family.

In the other family that reported problems in 1979, the source was also the physical disabilities of their transracially adopted 12-year-old son, who was diabetic and had "severe" learning disabilities and brain damage. The mother reported strains on the marriage as a result of the energy needed to cope with their son. The husband's parents had refused contact with the family for three and a half years because of the couple's decision to adopt transracially, although recently relations had improved. But even afterwards, the grandparents did not allow the adopted child to visit them in the small town in which they live, while continuing to invite both of their granddaughters who were born into the family. The parents forbade their daughters to go. The mother was also bitter because they were not told at the time of the adoption that the boy, who was then four years old, had brain damage and learning disabilities. She does not know whether these afflictions were inborn or acquired at the foster home where he had been placed. In 1984, the mother said that the family's recent move into a new house prevented them from participating in the study.

Two other families in the Minneapolis–St. Paul area who refused to participate told us that they were having problems now and were too tense to be interviewed. Looking back at their 1979 interviews, we found that in one of them we had noted that "the mother seems more tentative and more in need of answers than any other parent that I have talked with this far." The mother had said of her 8-year-old transracially adopted daughter: "I don't know how to enhance her self-image. I feel she is experiencing identity problems. I am white and feel frustrated because I wish I could encourage her positive blackness." She described her daughter as hyperactive and requiring special care, attention, and understanding. The mother also expressed regret about neglecting her 11-year-old biological son because of the attention demands of her daughter. In 1984, the father responded to our phone calls and said that the family had faced a number of problems and this was not a good time. When we phoned a few months later, the answer was still no.

The other family who reported problems in 1984 had 15 children, 5 of whom were adopted transracially. They adopted their last child in 1978 when he was eight years old. In 1979, one of the daughters born to them was recently divorced from her black husband, and she and her son lived in the parental home. Another daughter was married to a black. One of their transracially adopted sons, a native American married to an Apache woman, lived in Arizona. Another black son was planning to marry a white woman. In 1979 the mother described the family as follows: "Up until our last adoption everything was basically positive and good. All of the children go to Christian schools. Our newest son came with problems—lying, stealing, bed wetting, unable to learn.'' Toward the end of the interview the mother emphasized: ''We still believe in adoption and thank God for each of our 15 children. Yes, there have been tears and trials but through them all we have gone on and become better people. There has been a lot of joy and triumphs, too, and we are proud of this family of ours.''

The last three families who refused to participate had shown no signs of undue stress or strain in 1979. Two of them gave no reasons for their unwill-ingness to participate in 1984. The third family said that their transracially adopted son was not interested. ''He has been involved in too many such studies and was sick of them.'' At first the parents agreed to go ahead with-out him, but then decided that they were simply not ''that interested.''

In Chicago, the two families who refused to grant interviews gave no ex-planation save that they were ''too busy.'' An examination of their 1979 ques-tionnaires revealed that in one of the families the father had died in 1971, shortly before the first interview. There were nine children in that family, rang-ing in age from 24 to 2; the three oldest children were born into the family, the next four were white adoptees, and the last two were transracially adopted. In 1971 the transracially adopted son was 4 and the daughter 2. In 1979 the mother, who had recently remarried, described all the children as doing very well. She said of her black son that he is ''very brilliant, a superior student.'' Of her daughter, she observed, ''She has some scholastic problems; they are not major. She is a friendly child who is very well accepted by both black and white friends.''

The other Chicago family who did not agree to be interviewed had five children: three transracially adopted, two born to the parents. In 1979, both parents had made positive appraisals of their situation and of the children's relationships to each other and to them.

The 1979 profile of the St. Louis family who refused to participate in 1984 showed greater disagreement between the parents about what was happening to family relationships than we observed in most of the other families. The major discord revolved around their black adopted son who, at age 11, was the eldest of their three children. They had two daughters, aged 9 and 5, who were born to them. The mother reported that their son was being ''hassled by black peers for having white siblings and parents, and when we go down-town he tries to disassociate himself from us by walking behind us.'' She also told us that at school her daughters were often taunted by other blacks and that their brother did not stand up for them. The mother added that some of their black neighbors (they lived in an area that is half black, half white) were hostile toward them. She found it ''hard, confusing and disillusioning.'' The father, on the other hand, made no mention of these issues in his interview schedule, describing the family's situation in much more positive terms.

FAMILIES WHO REFUSED TO ALLOW
THEIR CHILDREN TO PARTICIPATE

There were six sets of parents who participated in the 1983–84 study but did not want to have their children interviewed. In the subsequent interview, the parents in one of the families described current problems that they believed stemmed from their decision to adopt. The other five sets of parents reported positive relations among family members and no problems with any of their children. None of the families were among those who were having problems in 1979.

The family who talked about their problems had a 17-year-old white adopted son, a 15-year-old black daughter, and an 11-year-old daughter born to them. The adopted daughter was at a correction center, charged with stealing and prostitution. When she was in the eighth grade she ran away from home for the first time, and over the next three years that had become a pattern.

In 1979, while generally describing family relations and their children's development in positive terms, the mother had characterized her then ten-year-old daughter as lacking self-control, as basically shy, and as "too often blamed if things among the siblings do not go well." She also reported that the child was an excellent student, got along well with peers and teachers, took flute, piano, and figure skating lessons, and belonged to the Camp Fire Girls. In addition, "She has a great deal of self confidence and many friends, most of whom are white, a few black." Neither the mother nor the father perceived their daughter as very conscious of her race: "She is a child of our family; she appears to be proud of her parents and her brother and sister and likes to go places with us."

Less than three years later, this same daughter began to run away repeatedly and to engage in serious acts of delinquency. The parents describe her as distrustful of everyone and manipulative of her younger sister. The parents attend a "support therapy group." At first they did not want to be interviewed either, but after a few follow-up phone calls, they changed their minds. The parents do not blame race, adoption, or themselves for their daughter's problems.

Of the remaining families who did not want their children to be interviewed, two were living in Chicago and two in St. Louis. The first of the Chicago families had four children; the two oldest, aged 19 and 16, were born to the parents; the next two were TRAs, a 14-year-old black daughter and an 11-year-old Indian/black son. The parents reported that they had had to seek help from the Human Relations Commission because they were harassed by their neighbors, who did not approve of their black children. They reported that they had had greater difficulty adopting their second child than their first because of the National Association of Black Social Workers' position on transracial adoption. But they persevered because they believed that their daughter needed a sibling of her own racial background. They might have considered a third transracial adoption, but the NABSW made the process too hard.

The second Chicago family had five children, three born to them, who were 25, 23, and 19 years old, and two transracially adopted black sons, 15 and 14 years old. The three oldest children were no longer living at home.

In the two St. Louis families who refused to allow their children to participate, each had two children born to them and two adopted nonwhite children. One of the families had also adopted two white children, and the other had been a foster family for two black children. In 1979, both families were sending their children to parochial schools, and the black transracial adoptees, according to the parents, saw themselves as black. Both families expressed no regrets about the adoptions and considered themselves blessed to have such lovely children and such positive relations among each other. In 1984, the parents in both families expressed the same sentiments. They rated their relations with all of their children positively; they emphasized that ''we dwell on the sameness amongst us and not on the differences.''

PROBLEM FAMILIES IN 1979,
IN 1979 AND 1983–84, AND IN 1983–84

In the 1979 phase of our study we described a group of families who evaluated their relations with at least one of their children as follows: ''The problems are such that the negative elements outweigh the positive ones,'' or ''The relationship is basically negative and bad.'' We also included families whose descriptions of their relations with their adopted children indicated serious problems stemming either from the adoption, from differences in race, or from both, even though they did not label themselves problem families. We said of those families:

> The most common episode related by the problem families is that of the adopted child stealing from his parents and siblings, being antagonistic and insulting toward them, and doing poorly in school. Most of these parents reported that siblings have had locks put on their bedroom doors to prevent the problem child from stealing money, clothing, and bikes. When confronted by the parents, the child typically lies, denies that he has taken the missing items and is abusive toward his parents or siblings. In almost every one of these families, the problem child is a male. His race, ordinal position in the family, or number of siblings does not seem to matter.
>
> Also common among the problem children were physical and/or mental or emotional disabilities. The parents believed these to be either genetic or the result of indifferent or abusive treatment in foster homes. The parents

expressed bitterness and resentment toward the adoption agency and the social workers, believing that they withheld information that might have influenced their decision to adopt that particular child. The third scenario is
less common than the first two but worthy of comment. Some parents expressed guilt at having inflicted harm on the biological child(ren) through their
decision to adopt transracially. They feared that the biological child(ren)
suffered neglect as a result of the time, energy, and attention that the adopted
child required due to some emotional or physical scar or handicaps. They also
noted that the family changed its life style in order to participate in the
adopted child's culture. Examples include families' moving into largely black
neighborhoods, joining a black church, trying to build a social life around
black friends, and observing and celebrating events in black history.[1]

Eleven of those 22 "problem" families participated in the current
study.[2] Of those 11, 4 no longer have serious problems resulting from the
adoption or from racial differences within the family. We describe briefly the
4 families who have apparently resolved the problems that they confronted in
1979.

For the first family, consisting of two parents and six children ranging
in age from 25 to 10, the focus of the problem in 1979 was their 12-year-old
black son. Five of the children had been born to the parents. In characteriz-
ing the quality of the relationship with their transracially adopted son, the
mother reported that the problems were such that "the negative elements out-
weighed the positive ones." They adopted their son when he was 20 months
old, before which he had been in a foster home. The parents reported that
the boy had no friends and that he was spaced out.

> He has problems with his adoption. He doesn't understand why he was given
> away. The family is always picking up after him. Siblings had to toe the line
> and they resent the fact that the adopted sibling gets away with laxity. There
> is resentment between the siblings because there are repeated incursions into
> their privacy; he does things to indicate that he is simply out of it.

The mother also reported that her two daughters had married blacks and
that their biological son was dating a black girl. One of the marriages was a
disaster. "The husband was into drugs, they got a divorce, there is one child
out of that marriage." The mother still saw transracial adoption as a fulfillment of her values, but she blamed the adoption agency for inadequate screen-
ing and for having given them insufficient information.

Five years later, in 1984, the parents reported that if they had an opportunity to begin again, they would do nothing differently. All things being
equal, they believe that it is better to place children with families who share
their racial backgrounds or culture; but "the fact is there are more black children available for adoption than there are black families willing or able to

adopt.'' The 12-year-old TRA son is now a junior in high school, with average grades between C- and D. He plans to go to college and major in physical education and play sports. The parents report that he is a ''good mixer'' and gets along well with his 20-year-old and 15-year-old sisters, who are still living at home. The parents now evaluate their relationship with him as ''having problems but the positive elements outweigh the negative ones.'' They continue to view him as self-centered and wish that he was ''more tuned in to other people's existence.'' The parents report that their son considers himself black, but a ''suburban black,'' like his brother-in-law.

Looking at the responses of the child in question, his score on the Family Integration Scale is 13, which is lower than the average and indicates high family integration. On the self-esteem scale, his score is 16, which shows higher self-esteem than the average. The boy expects to be close to his family, both to his parents and his siblings. They are, in his words, ''my family; of course I want to be close, I want to know what's going on.'' Concerning his future, he commented as follows:

> I hope I live somewhere like this, except more mixed so my kids can learn that all races are the same.... I hope I have a good job and make good money.... I'll probably marry a black girl; they aren't as hyperactive and dizzy as white girls.... I probably won't participate in any black organizations. I'm not a hard worker. If I'm in a group I would be expected to carry some of the load and I probably won't. I usually don't have time for stuff like that.

The second family was composed of seven people: the mother and father, three daughters aged 21, 19, and 16, one son born to them who was 18, and one transracially adopted son who was 17. The two oldest daughters do not live in the community. The 16-year-old daughter was not available when the rest of the family was interviewed. In 1979, the parents had dwelled on the behavior of their adopted son; he was stealing from both his parents and siblings and destroying family property. He did not work in school, disrupted classes, and demanded to be the center of attention. The parents said of their relationship with him, ''The problems are such that the negative elements outweigh the positive ones.'' But they went on to describe themselves as ''working as a team in trying to solve their problems.''

Sometimes between 1979 and 1984, the adopted son, his brother, and the youngest daughter ended up in an alcohol treatment center. The sons spent two years away from home living at the center, undergoing a highly disciplined reform program. The parents did not refer to this episode, but both sons discussed their experiences at the center and expressed pride in the fact that they and their sister ''graduated'' from it and were now on the ''right path.''

During the 1984 interview, the adopted son answered the question "Are there some qualities about you that you think are special?" by commenting: "Being adopted, especially being picked by my parents. Getting along well with others, understanding how people feel." He reported that his average grade last year was a C, but he hoped to go to college, where he would like to learn how to be a restaurant chef. His self-esteem score was 15, indicating higher than average self-esteem. On the family integration scale, his score of 12 also demonstrated higher than average integration.

All five of his close friends are white, and they all had participated in the alcohol treatment program. He and his brother attend Alcoholics Anonymous (AA) meetings on a regular basis. Of his future relations with his family, he expects to be close to his parents, his brother, and his younger sister, but not to his older sisters, with whom, he says, he never had a close relationship. He would not guess about the type of community in which he might live or the type of person he might marry. Participation in black organizations is of no interest to him. He would like to find out who his birth parents are and plans to pursue that issue when he is older.

The son born into the family answered the question about his special qualities with: "The care I have for others, understanding and awareness of myself and others; pride in myself and my family relationships." Like his brother, his close friends are also previous residents of the treatment center, and he reports spending much of his free time with AA activities. His self-esteem score of 14 shows high self-esteem, and his family integration score of 9 shows very high integration. It is clear from the interview that his identity as a graduate of the treatment center is important to him and that his previous experiences are sources of shame. He expects to remain close to his parents and to his siblings, especially the two who were at the alcohol treatment center with him. At the end of the interview he commented: "I never liked being in a mixed family before because I didn't have pride in myself. Anyone can be happy with what they are as long as they're happy with themselves. I have a lot of family pride. Even though L is adopted, he's my brother."

The parents made no mention of the alcohol problem in their interview. Of course, given their willingness to allow their sons to be interviewed (and their acceptance of the conditions of privacy), they must have assumed that their sons would talk about their experiences. The parents reported that they expected to be close to their sons. Of the brothers' relations to each other, they commented, "Before 23 months ago, they were angry and abusive toward each other; now they have a caring, loving brotherly relationship." And about the future they said: "They will have a strong relationship. They will have close ties because of what they went through." (That last phrase is the only mention the parents made of the experiences described by the sons.) The parents answered most of the other items with one or two words. Yet they expressed no reluctance in granting the interview or involving their children. Maybe they were worn out, or holding their breath, or simply taciturn. Reading the sons' interviews, one feels that they were optimistic and that they felt good about themselves and their ties to each other.

The third family's problems in 1979 centered around the jealousy and insecurity felt by one of the children born into the family toward her Korean adopted brother and especially toward her Korean sister. Both of the children were adopted when they were six years old. The two children born into the family were nine (the oldest son) and eight (the daughter who had the problems) when the adoptions took place. The daughter had left home and moved to the West Coast for a few years, but had recently returned. In her interview she talked about getting her life together, going back to school, not drinking, and coming to terms with feelings about her sister.

The adopted sister described anger at her Korean mother for giving her up for adoption and a desire to look like the other people in her adopted family. She was jealous of her sister's blond hair. She experienced lots of name calling—"Pearl Harbor," "chink," "gook"—and some children used to spit at her. She went through a period of dependency on drugs (alcohol, pot, LSD) and stayed in a residential treatment center. The parents traced their adopted daughter's problem to her anger at her biological mother for giving her up and for earning a living by prostitution. What came through most clearly in the 1984 interviews was the closeness, the mutual dependency that both sisters felt toward each other, and the hopefulness on the part of the parents that the worst was over for both daughters.

In the fourth family, both parents had died (the father in 1966 and the mother in 1975). There were five children: three were born to the parents, and two were transracially adopted. In 1979, the daughter born into the family answered the questionnaire as a parent surrogate. In 1984, she and the two TRA daughters were living in the family home. The oldest daughter still plays a maternal role to her two TRA siblings, viewing herself as their mother. The brothers in the family play tangential roles. By 1983, the oldest daughter had completed four years of college and was planning to go on for her master's degree. She was hopeful that both of her sisters would also finish college and be self-sufficient, although she reported that the 19-year-old has a learning disability. The 19-year-old TRA has an especially close relationship with the 21-year-old sister, whom she describes as her second mother. The two sisters who participated in the survey expect to hold the family together.

We turn next to the seven families in the 1984 survey who reported problems in 1979 and who continued to report serious problems. In six of the seven families, the major problem reported in the 1979 survey was stealing by the transracially adopted child from other family members. The seventh family was the one that we described as "tragic" in both the 1971 and 1979 studies because the daughter was diagnosed as having phenylketonuria (PKU).

In all but one of these families, the children who had had problems in

1979 were no longer living at home. In five of the families, the parents had placed the child in a drug rehabilitation center, a psychiatric hospital, or were under court order to send their child to a juvenile facility. In the sixth family, the son had left the area when he was 17 and moved to the Southwest, where he is currently working and married.

In six of the seven families, the problems with the TRA child had repercussions for the other children in the family. They felt neglected by their parents because of the energy and time it took to relate to the "problem child." Later they felt deceived because their parents made decisions and took actions involving their sibling without discussing it with them, or even informing them ahead of time, for example, placing their brother or sister in a drug therapy center or a hospital. One of the children born into the family developed a serious eating disorder (anorexia nervosa) which she attributes to lack of parental attention.

All of the TRA children in the six families who had stolen from other family members had been adopted when they were between four and seven years old. Two were American black; the others were native Americans and Korean. All had been in foster homes or institutionalized before the adoption; all had mental or physical handicaps. In all but one family, the parents and the siblings emphasized that the racial differences were *not* the cause or source of the problem; the child's early history and physical/mental disability were, in their view, the important factors.

The one family who did consider race important lived in a "village" outside the larger community where most of the interviews were conducted, and the parents felt that their son was "too different. He needed to go somewhere where he did not stand out, where he could get lost in the crowd." He is the child mentioned above who moved to the Southwest and married a white woman.

The three families who had adopted an American Indian used to attend pow-wows, prepared ethnic food, and had Indian books and artifacts in their home, but the children showed no interest. In one of the families, a TRA son who was 14 in 1984 was still stealing from his parents and lying to them.

With one exception, the seven sets of parents expect and hope that "things will get better" and that the children will feel positively toward each other and toward them. There are indications in five of the families that the parents and the TRA child with the difficulties are indeed working through their problems. But the children born into those families do not trust their parents and do not expect to have a close relationship with them. They are bitter and angry. Another TRA son (the one who is still living at home) has built walls between himself and his parents and siblings that may be difficult or impossible to penetrate. In the one family where the parents (primarily the father) are negative, the TRA son believes that adopting children after they are two or three years old makes "bonding" difficult and unlikely; and the problems only get worse.

Although we placed the family with the daughter who has PKU in the "problems in 1979 and problems in 1984" category, the family perceives itself as being in much better shape now than it was five years ago. The daughter is living in a group home, and she is able to return to the parental home for brief visits without causing turmoil. The three children born into the family have more positive feelings toward her and their parents than they did five years ago. The parents are now hopeful that "S" may eventually be able to earn a living and look after herself. Five years ago, they were doubtful of that possibility. Each of the children describes scars resulting from "S's" adoption, but they are nevertheless more positive toward their parents than are children in the other "problem" families. Unlike the latter children, they do not blame their parents for "S."

In the last category are the nine families who were having serious problems when we interviewed them in 1984, but had not reported difficulties in 1979. In addition, we included two "problem" families whom we could not locate in 1979, but found in 1984.

In 3 of the 11 families, the parents are divorced—a much higher rate than the five divorces and three separations reported in the remaining 85 families. Among the three, the mother has custody of all six children in one family, the father has custody of all four children in the second family, and in the third family the mother has custody of three of the four children. The father has custody of the transracially adopted son.

The parents in the family where the mother has custody of all six children were divorced in 1976. The two youngest children, 15- and 14-year-old sons, are transracially adopted. The oldest of the children born into the family is 24. The 14-year-old transracial adoptee has a severe learning disability; he cannot read or write and attends a special school. He also has a drug problem, and the family has a history of alcoholism. According to the mother, she, the father, who is a physician, and the second child born to them, now 20 years old, are all alcoholics. The mother is a lesbian whose lover lives with her and the children. The older of the two TRAs is very self-conscious about being black. He described experiences of people staring at the family when they are in restaurants, stores, and other public places. He believes that he would fit in better in his family, his neighborhood, and his school if he were white. Most of his friends are white. He commented: "I don't act like I'm black. . . . Yes, I would prefer to be white, so I wouldn't be stared at and because I act like I am white."

The youngest son also noted that "people look at you funny when we are out as a family," but seemed unconcerned about his blackness or about his difference from the family because of race. He talked more about having been "shuffled back and forth" between his mother's and father's home when he was younger and his learning disability. He could not remember any incident when someone was nasty to him because of his racial background. For all of the unusual arrangements in this family, the mother and children refer to each other warmly and generously. The children's family integration scores were average, and they all expected to be close to their mother, though not to each other.

In the second divorced family, the mother had had custody of all four children (the oldest daughter, 17, and the youngest son, 13, who were born to the parents, and the two middle sons, 15 and 14, who were transracially adopted) until a few months prior to the interview, when the father gained custody of the 15-year-old black son, who has a learning disability and problems in school, where his average grade last year was a D. Early in the interview the mother expressed resentment at the boy, explaining that she might have found it easier to remarry if she did not have him. He produced great strains on her and stress in the family because of his immature, loud, attention-seeking, demanding behavior. The mother also reported poor relations between that child and his siblings. In addition to his learning disability, the boy is small for his age, and the mother feels that his size has caused him more problems than his color. His adopted black brother, who is one year younger, is tall and expects to play college and professional basketball. The divorce also, she believes, affected the TRA with the disability more than the other children. Both of the adopted sons consider themselves black and plan to live in black or mixed communities. At the end of the interview, in reflecting on the family and the decision to adopt black children, the mother said she felt that the adoption had been good for "Y" and "L" (the two children born to her). It had "allowed them to reach beyond stereotypes and judge people as people, not on the basis of race. As adults, they will have gotten a complex and enriching experience."

All of the children's interviews bore out the mother's account. The black son, who now lives with his father, talked a lot about his size and his strength. In his self-description he characterized himself, in his order: "short, not white, curly hair, jeans, tennis shoes." In response to the question about special qualities, he said, "I'm small and have lots of muscles for my size." He received an award for doing "the hardest stuff" in gymnastics. Unlike the other three children, he emphasized his closeness to his father, and on the last item on the Family Integration Scale ("My parents know what I am really like as a person") he checked "disagree" for Mom and "agree" for Dad.

He does not expect to have a close relationship with his mother in the future: "She doesn't understand a lot of things. I say things and she mixes them up." His father "does understand how I feel." He expects to live in a "mixed" community and will probably marry a black person, because "I'd feel more comfortable." He does not expect to participate in black organizations because "I was never into any of that stuff."

The father was also interviewed, and the responses reflect his closeness to the son who is living with him. When asked how he felt about the position of the Black Social Workers, the father said: "I told them right back what I thought. That what blacks do to prepare kids for a hostile system is wrong. They make a lot out of nothing." The father sees whatever problems "O" has as stemming from the conflict between himself and his ex-wife. He anticipates a warm/close relationship with "O" as "O" continues to live with him as well as after he leaves his home.

In the third divorced family, the father has had custody of all four children since the divorce in 1973. The mother no longer lives in the state. Of the four children, the two oldest (daughters, 19 and 17) were born into the family and the two youngest (sons, 15 and 14) were transracially adopted. The 15-year-old has a learning disability; "he was kicked out of high school" last year. The father describes him as "very self centered. The whole world revolves around him"; the boy does not get along with his siblings, and the father rates his own relationship with him as a "3." (The problems are such that the negative elements outweigh the positive ones.) The heart of the problem stems from the boy's mother (the ex-wife) who, according to the father, suffered a "severe depression" when "C," the 15-year-old black adopted son, was between 2 and 5 years old. During her depression, he stated, she would say directly to "C," "I hate you," and tell the other children how she felt about him. The mother's rejection has continued to the present and is evidenced in the absence of any relationship between them. On the day of the interview, for instance, the mother was in town and took her daughters and youngest TRA son out for the afternoon, but "C" was not invited. He receives no birthday or Christmas presents from her as the others do. "C" is in therapy now. The father says that he is maturing very slowly and "it may take 20 or 30 years before he is independent."

"C" describes his own projections about his future ties to his family as follows:

> If I don't change, then things will be the same as they are now, which is I wouldn't call them up and talk to them. If I change, then I would get in touch with them. But I don't know if I will. Now we don't get along. I'm not as responsible as they want me to be. I feel happy being the way I am now. They don't like it. If I mature more, which is doubtful, then I'll have responsibility and we'll get along better.

Regarding other aspects of his future, he said: "If I become rich I'll move in with the rich people. By then you never know who is going to be rich, which color is going to be rich. It could be the Vietnamese." He has already chosen the girl whom he plans to marry; she is white and Catholic. He acknowledges that his girlfriend's parents are not happy about their relationship. "C" told the interviewers at the beginning of the interview that his mother was visiting and had taken out only his sisters and brother. He said that he hated her.

The other son is a good student (B to B + average grades), enjoys sports and music, has a good relationship with his sisters and parents, identifies himself as white, and aspires to live in a "nice, white suburban community and marry a middle class white girl."

Among the remaining eight families, all of whom are intact, there are four in which the parents describe some problems with one or more of their children. But the children, while they admit that there are some difficulties, generally draw a positive family profile and report that they anticipate close and positive ties to their parents and siblings in the future. For example, in one family with a 17-year-old TRA daughter as the only child, the parents are "desperate about her drinking at parties and her poor performance in school." In 1979, this was a family who talked about their daughter in glowing terms. She was a gifted student, musician, and skater. The parents trace their daughter's subsequent problems to her feelings of abandonment by her birth mother. They would no longer recommend TRA to anyone. In contrast, interviewing their daughter was like talking about another family. She described close and strong relationships with her parents, acknowledged that her behavior did not meet their standards, but viewed this as a "bad period" that they were all going through and that would improve. They were her parents; she expects to be close to them always.

A similar theme emerged in three of the other "problem" families. The parents made negative, harsh assessments about the quality of their relationships with their children and expressed the feeling that the adoption had been a mistake. Although the children reported problems, they also described positive, warm, upbeat feelings toward their parents and toward each other.

In one of those families, the parents said: "Racial problems were brought into our home every evening. Everything was fine until N was 14, then he needed black role models which we could not provide for him. The Black Social Workers are right. It's too hard on the kids living in a white family." But the 19-year-old black son in question did not share his parents' pessimism. He felt good about his relationship with them, while recognizing that there have been, and still are, problems.

In the fourth such family, one of the TRA sons (now 20 years old), had run away from home and had become involved with a family who trained children to carry out robberies. He is a child with a severe learning disability who cannot read or write. He has two TRA siblings and one brother who was born to the parents. Again, the children all have positive feelings toward each other, toward their parents, and toward the family as a unit. The parents sound exhausted.

In the remaining four problem families, a different pattern emerges: one or two TRA children, out of many others in the family, are angry, hostile, bitter, and anxious to separate themselves from the family. In one family of 14 children, of whom 3 are transracially adopted, the 2 youngest TRA daughters, 17 and 15 years old, describe a lack of trust in the family, a belief that their parents would not stick by them, and anger at the rude behavior exhibited by their parents toward their friends. The 2 children born to the parents who are still at home shared none of their siblings' perspectives.

The same pattern appears in a family of four children, three of whom are TRAs, but only the 18-year-old daughter, who dropped out of school when she was 14 and has been arrested for prostitution, assault, and shoplifting, is angry and wants out. In another family, one of the TRA daughters is in a correctional facility for shoplifting and prostitution. The daughter, who is 15, started running away from home periodically when she was in the eighth grade. According to the parents, the other children, who include TRAs and those born into the family, do not engage in antisocial behavior and seem to have positive, close ties to their parents and siblings.

In the last of the 1984 problem families, the oldest of two Vietnamese adopted daughters left home and is living with her boyfriend, whose family takes care of their expenses. She is 17 years old and attending high school. The parents have not spoken to her in several months. They described her as having a "borderline personality." The clinical psychologist to whom they had taken her several years ago told them, "Her self concept is poor; she becomes confused easily, is subject to emotional outbursts and is unable to properly label her emotions." The parents described positive experiences with their 15-year-old Vietnamese adopted daughter and with their two older sons, who were born to them. The sons share their parents' feelings, but the 15-year-old daughter does not. She has closed herself off from her parents (but not from her brothers and her sister, whom she sees without her parents' knowledge.) The younger daughter does not believe that her parents understand her or her sister, to whom she is sympathetic. About her parents, she hopes that "perhaps, in the future, I will find it easier to talk with them."

In sum, we have found that 18 of the 96 families are experiencing serious problems. Among 7 of them, the problems are long-standing, going back at least five years. They manifested themselves initially when the transracially adopted child began to steal from parents and siblings. None of those children are living at home. They have been placed in drug rehabilitation centers, psychiatric hospitals, or juvenile facilities. In 1 family, the son left on his own when he was 17. The children were all adopted when they were at least 4 years old and had serious mental and/or physical handicaps at the time. They had lived in foster homes or public institutions prior to their adoption. The parents, with one exception, emphasized that in their view race was not the source of the child's difficulties. They focused instead on the child's experiences in the institutions and on the child's disabilities. The parents are still hopeful that the child will overcome those problems and that they will have a positive relationship with the child.

Three of the 11 families whose problems were reported to us for the first time in the 1984 interviews are divorced. Some of the children's problems stem from the parents' relationship; but learning disabilities and other developmental problems are also reported for the children in these families.

There are two patterns in the eight other problem families. In one group, the parents portrayed their problems and their sense of estrangement from their transracially adopted child in harsher, more negative terms than those used by the child or the siblings to describe the relationship. Some of these parents did attribute their problems with the child to racial differences. They were hurt, disappointed, and pessimistic. The children, on the other hand, characterize much of what they are experiencing as a phase or bad period. In the long run, the adopted children believe the relationship with their parents will be a good one.

In the second group, most of the children, those adopted and those born into the family, and the parents feel positively toward each other. One child has engaged in delinquent behavior or has rejected the family's rules and left. These parents, like many of the others, do not trace the source of the problems to the child's racial background. They emphasize instead developmental and personality characteristics. They also point out that their other transracially adopted child has not engaged in antisocial behavior.

Having drawn in some detail a negative, harsh portrait of these 18 families, we turn next to the much larger category of "ordinary" families.

NOTES

1. Rita J. Simon and Howard Altstein, *Transracial Adoption: A Follow-up* (Lexington, Mass.: Lexington Books, 1981), pp. 29-30.

2. Among the 11 families who did not participate, 7 moved out of areas where it would have been feasible to conduct the interviews, and 4 refused.

8

Ordinary Families: A Collective Portrait

The previous chapter described all of the bruises, warts, and ugliness we discovered in the families who were experiencing problems. Some of the vignettes portrayed deceit, ignorance, and lack of trust between parents and children, between the adopted children and the children born into the family, and between adopted siblings. We reported anger, disgust, lack of communication, and indifference by persons in each of these categories. We have to assume that the reader has been affected by those accounts and wonders about the wisdom and practicality of transracial adoption. The collective portrait that we draw in this chapter is not meant to disavow the facts described in the "problem families," but it is intended to depict the dominant themes, the life patterns, the emotions, and the interactions among the majority—indeed, among at least four out of five of all the families in the study. This picture was developed after reading all of the parents' and children's interviews and examining the tables derived from the descriptive statistics.

In journalism, it is "bad news"—catastrophes, tragedies, both human and naturally induced—that sell newspapers, make headlines, keep listeners glued to their radios and TV sets. But in science, we are more interested in the major trends, in the larger patterns, in what seem to be the predominant themes, without of course discarding the deviant cases. Thus, what we did in the previous chapter was to provide the reader with all the information we could glean from our data about the difficulties our families were confronting and the ways in which they were responding to these problems.

This chapter looks at the "ordinary families." We believe that the portrait that emerges is a positive, warm, integrated picture that shows parents and children who feel good about themselves and about their relationships with each other. On the issue of transracial adoption, almost all of the parents would do it again and would recommend it to other families. They believe that they and the children born to them have benefitted from their experiences. Their birth children have developed insight, sensitivity, and a tolerance that they could not have acquired in the ordinary course of life. Their transracial adoptees may have been spared years in foster homes or institutions. They have had the comfort and security of loving parents and siblings who have provided them with a good home, education and cultural opportunities, and the belief that they are wanted.

We found that almost all of the families made some changes in their lives as a result of their decision to adopt. Most of the time, however, the changes were not made because of their decision to adopt a child of a different race, but because they decided to add another child to the family. Thus, the parents talked about buying a bigger house, adding more bedroom space, having less money for vacations and entertainment, and allowing less time for themselves. In retrospect, most of the parents do not dwell on what they wished they had done but did not do; nor do they berate themselves for things they did and wished they had not done. Most of them feel that they did their best. They worked hard at being parents and at being parents of children of a different race.

In the early years, many of them were enthusiastic about introducing the culture of the TRAs' backgrounds into the family's day-to-day life. This was especially true of the families who adopted American Indian and Korean children. They experimented with new recipes; sought out books, music, and artifacts; joined churches and social organizations; travelled to the Southwest for ceremonies; and participated in local ethnic events. The parents of black children primarily introduced books about black history and black heroes, joined a black church, sought out black playmates for their children, and celebrated Martin Luther King's birthday. In a few families, a black friend is the godparent to their TRA child. One mother told us: "Black parents regard us as black parents."

But as the years wore on, as the children became teenagers and pursued their own activities and social life, the parents' enthusiasm and interest for "ethnic variety" waned. An increasing number of families lived as their middle and upper middle class white neighbors did. Had the children shown more interest, more desire to maintain ethnic contacts and ties, most of the parents would have been willing to follow the same direction; but in the absence of signals that the activities were meaningful to their children, the parents decided that the one-culture family was an easier route. Almost all of the parents said that they were affected by the stance of the National Association of Black Social Workers and that of the Native American Councils in the 1970s vis-a-vis the adoption of blacks and Indian children by white families. Almost all of the parents thought that the position taken by those groups was contrary to the best interests of the child and smacked of racism. They were angered by the accusations of the Black Social Workers that white parents could not rear black children, and they felt betrayed by groups whose respect they expected they would have. "Race," they believed, was not and should not be an important criterion for deciding a child's placement. In their willingness to adopt, they were acting in the best interest of a homeless, neglected, unwanted child. One parent said: "Our children are the ones no one wanted. Now they are saying you are the wrong family."

Some (a handful) parents felt guilty as a result of the attacks on them, and that guilt resulted in their decision not to adopt a second or, in some instances, a third nonwhite child. "Perhaps," some of them said, "the position of the Black Social Workers is right." They had ventured into a far more complicated social world than the one for which they were prepared. Good will and the desire to have and love a child (or another child) were not sufficient reasons for adopting someone for whom they could not provide the desired or necessary racial or ethnic heritage. Among this handful, some said that they could understand "their [the Black Social Workers] position because our kids have white values." Others among this small group said: "We are not and cannot be appropriate black role models. We've learned that is important." But, we emphasize, only a handful of parents made those observations.

While almost all of the parents felt that they had been affected one way or another by the Black Social Workers' position, practically none of them believed that it had any effect on their children, primarily because the children were too young to hear about and understand the issues.

While we have said this earlier, we think this observation bears reemphasis: namely, our sense of the respondents' (both the parents' and the children's) candor and honesty in describing their feelings, their hopes, their disappointments, and their regrets. At no time during the interviews did this come through more clearly than in the families' evaluations of the quality of their relationships with each other, and their assessments of the relationships between other members of the family. In their responses to our request to characterize their relationship with each child on a scale of one to four—"basically positive and good" to "basically negative and bad"—the mothers and fathers talked out their feelings, evaluated the pros and cons in their relationships, compared the past few years to the present, and then came up with an answer. In most instances, when the mother and father were participating in the interview together, they presented a joint evaluation, but not always; there were families in which the mothers and fathers disagreed. There was no consistent pattern that would limit more negative evaluations to one parent rather than the other. Where there were disagreements between the parents, however, it was never by more than one position on the scale.

The parents went through the same detailed, historical analyses when they were asked to evaluate the quality of the relationships among their children. The majority were willing to explore their children's personalities, strengths, and weaknesses in great detail.

On the whole, as the data reported in Chapter 4 show, the evaluations were positive, but there were more "2's" (i.e., there are problems, but the positive elements outweigh the negative ones) than "1's" (i.e., the relationship is basically positive and good). There was no consistent pattern in their evaluation of the children born to them as opposed to those whom they adopted, nor in their judgments about the relationships between siblings born into the family and those adopted. The parents emphasized "interests," "tastes," "age differences," "jealousy," "competitiveness." The adoptive status of the child was not a prime determinant of those qualities or feelings, according to the parents.

The children answered the questions posed to them about their relationship to family members with the same frankness and honesty that was apparent among the parents. We noted earlier that, somewhat to our surprise, in many families the children made more positive evaluations of the quality of their family relationships than did the parents. The parents, in some instances, seemed willing to step back and disengage themselves from the situation; the children—and here we have to take special note of the TRAs—continually said: "They are my parents. Yeah, we've had our differences, but I know I can count on them and I want to be close." That is not meant to indicate that many of the older ones (those in their late teens) were not anxious and ready to move out of the parental home; they were. But the TRAs unequivocally did not perceive their relationships with their parents as temporary or transitional. Practically none of them, even those who expressed anger and bitterness about their current relations, said that they were likely to cut off ties completely or walk out of the family.

We did not find the same type of commitment among the siblings. But, here again, it is important to stress that negative or indifferent feelings were not restricted to the relationships between adopted and born into the family siblings. As in the case of the parents' judgments, the siblings' evaluations were based on personality characteristics, interests, tastes, age differences, sex, talents, and prior history, not adoptive status.

One topic that seemed to have been exhausted by the third phase of our study was the quality of the TRAs' relationships with other relatives—grandparents, aunts, uncles, and cousins. No parent reported that their TRA children had been rejected or that ties had been severed by the grandparents or other relatives. In many families, one or more of the grandparents had died, or grandparents and other relatives lived too far away to make frequent contact feasible; but there were also numerous families in which the children talked warmly about their vacations at grandparents' homes, their visits with aunts, uncles, and cousins, and their sense of family ties. We rarely heard TRAs describe situations in which they felt rejected by their extended family members. Large family gatherings, however, were most likely to provoke awareness by the TRAs of the differences in appearance between them and the rest of their relatives. It was on these occasions that they were most likely to wish that the differences did not exist. But for the most part, adoption meant membership in the extended family unit, according to both parents and children.

Much of what we have portrayed thus far has been gleaned from the perceptions and opinions of the parents. And there is still more to be said from that vantage point, especially about the future. But let us briefly turn away from the parents and begin drawing the children's collective portrait. There are two major thrusts to our comments about the children. First, we demonstrate that the children born into the families and the TRAs resemble each other far more than they differ in their tastes and interests, educational aspirations, choice of friends, and feeling about their parents. Second, we characterize what is distinctive about being black or Indian or Korean in a white family, in a largely white neighborhood, and assess whether that distinctiveness has made a difference for better or worse.

We wrote earlier at some length about the uses of the Self-Esteem Scale, its meaning, and the scores achieved by black and white adolescents in the Baltimore school system and other areas. The Rosenberg and Simmons study reported consistently higher self-esteem (meaning lower scores) for black children than for whites in the same grade and school system. It also reported that the crucial factor in determining self-esteem was the role of "significant others." That is, the respondents' views of the assessments made by their friends, classmates, teachers, and mothers heavily influenced their own self-esteem.

We applied the same scale to the adolescents in our study and found no differences by race or adoptive status. Because we wanted to make the best possible comparison between our respondents and those included in the Rosenberg and Simmons study, we examined the scores of our black TRAs separately from those of the other TRAs and from those of the white born and white adopted children. The scores for all four groups were virtually the same. No one category manifested higher or lower self-esteem than the others.

The lack of difference among our respondents on the Self-Esteem Scale reminds us of the lack of difference we reported for these children in the first study when we asked them to choose dolls of different races. A child received one point each time he or she selected the white doll in response to: "Which doll would you: (a) like to play with the best? (b) think is a nice doll? (c) think is a nice color?" and did not select the white doll as the doll that looked bad. The scores obtained demonstrated that none of the children manifested a white racial preference. Out of a possible score of 4, which would have meant that the white doll was selected in response to each question, the average score was 1.7. This indicated that none of the children selected the white dolls even half the time.

On the basis of all the responses to the items in which dolls were used to measure racial attitudes, racial awareness, and racial identity, we found no consistent differences among the adopted and nonadopted children and among the black and other transracially adopted children. We wrote in our first volume:

> There was no consistent preference for the white doll among the black, white, and Indian or Oriental children. There was no indication that the black children had acquired racial awareness earlier than the white children, and there was no evidence that the white children were able to identify themselves more accurately than the nonwhite children.[1]

Our 1972 study was the first to report that there were no white racial preferences among American black and white children. The responses suggested that the unusual family environment in which these children were being reared might have caused their deviant racial attitudes and resulted in their not sharing with other American children a sense that white is preferable to other races. We noted that the children's responses also demonstrated that their deviant racial attitudes did not affect their ability to identify themselves accurately.

Both sets of responses, those obtained in 1972 and in 1984, consistently portray a lack of difference between black and white children in these special, multiracial families, when differences have been and continue to be present between black and white children reared in the usual single-racial family. We emphasize in this writing, as we did in the 1977 volume, that something special seems to happen to both black and white children when they are reared together as siblings in the same family.

The lack of differences among our adolescent responses is again dramatically exemplified in our findings on the Family Integration Scale. The hypothesis was that adopted children would feel less integrated than children born into the families. But the scores reported by our four groups of respondents (black TRAs, other TRAs, white born, and white adopted) showed no significant differences and, indeed, among the three largest categories (not including the white adoptees), the mean scores measuring family integration were practically identical: 15.4, 15.2, and 15.4

Looking for additional indicators of the extent to which the adopted as opposed to the nonadopted respondents felt that they were integrated into the family, we examined responses to items asking to whom they would go if they were happy about something, worried about something, wrongly accused of stealing, and whom they thought really knew best what they were like as a person. On these items as well, we found no differences by adoptive status. But one pattern did emerge that warrants comment: the differences in responses between daughters and sons.

In their study of transracial adoption in England, Gill and Jackson found that the girls scored better than the boys on the Family Integration Scale (i.e., their responses showed that they felt more integrated into their family than did the boys).[2] Our item-by-item examination revealed a small but consistent tendency for the TRA daughters to feel *less* integrated than the TRA sons. There was no such pattern among the sons and daughters born into the families. Similarly, on the items asking "who would you tell," the TRA daughters were consistently *less* likely to select a parent than were the TRA sons, or the sons and daughters born into the family. The differences were even smaller on the "expected closeness" to parents and siblings in the future, but on these items as well, the TRA daughters signalled that they did not anticipate seeking out either their parents or their siblings to the extent indicated by the children in the other categories. One explanation for these differences is that the girls feel the rejection by their birth mothers more keenly than the boys do, and as a result are less trusting of their adoptive parents.

Turning to the matter of perceptions about race and racial identities, we reported that 71 percent of the transracial adoptees said that they had no problem with the fact that they were the only black or Korean or Indian person in the family. By the time of our study, they simply took it for granted. And the same percentages of TRAs as white children answered "No" to the item that asked, "Have there been times in your life when you wished you were another color?" We did find, however, that when we asked them to identify themselves so that someone whom they had never met would recognize them at a meeting place, many more of TRAs than white children mentioned race. Such a choice, though, may have more to do with the practicalities of the situation than with any sense of "affect" or evaluation. If one is black or Korean or Indian in a largely white area, recognition is much easier.

Eleven percent of the TRAs told us directly that they would prefer to be white, and 27 percent of the parents believe that their TRAs identify themselves as white. According to the parents, all of these children are of mixed backgrounds. The parents' responses on such matters as their children's choice of friends, dates, interests, aspirations, and so on, demonstrate that they are knowledgeable about and understand their children's thoughts, activities, and tastes.

Thus, the above mentioned discrepancy between the children and the parents concerning the former's racial identity should not be assumed to represent the parents' lack of insight or recognition regarding their children's beliefs and desires. Some part of that 27 percent of parents who believe that their TRAs identify themselves as white could well reflect wish fulfillment by the parents. Most of those children look as if they are white; the parents might like to believe that the children also consider themselves to be white, like the rest of the family. Some evidence for this hypothesis may be seen in the parents' and adolescents' estimates about the adolescents' future. For example, a greater number of TRAs said that they would opt to live in a racially mixed community than did parents, more of whom thought the TRAs would chose to live in a community like the one in which they were reared (predominantly white). Interestingly, about 25 percent of both the parents and children thought the children would marry exogamously. Thus, the evidence we have for parental ambivalence over having a child of a different race is the 16 percent difference between the parents' and adolescents' responses on the item about racial identity, together with the expectations on the part of more TRAs than parents that the former would live in racially mixed rather than predominantly white communities. Neither of these issues, however, is directly tied to the sense of integration or cohesion felt by the parents and children about their relationship.

We found that parents and children saw eye to eye on two other "race" related issues. First, we reported that 60 percent of the parents and 65 percent of the adolescents told us that they talked about race, including racial differences, racial attitudes, and racial discrimination, in their homes. Both parents and adolescents also agreed that the context for most of the discussions involved the families' and children's friends, activities at school, and community events. The next most often cited context concerned political figures, with Jesse Jackson most frequently mentioned. (Remember that many of the interviews were conducted during the 1984 presidential campaign.) The third most popular context involved stories on TV and in the newspapers. The children born into the families were more likely to report discussions of race than were the TRAs.

A second topic on which there was strong agreement between parents and children concerned the extent to which the TRAs encountered nasty or unpleasant experiences because of their race. Sixty-five percent of the parents and 67 percent of the TRAs reported at least one such incident. Both the parents and their children agreed that most of these occurrences involved name calling—"nigger," "jungle bunny," "chink," "gook," etc. About 10 percent in both groups described incidents in which, in the opinion of the children and the parents, a teacher or a parent of a friend made insulting, racist remarks. The majority of the adolescents did not seem to be deeply affected by their encounters; temporary anger, more than hurt, was their main reaction. The parents reported talking to the child about the experience, and in some instances going to the school or the parent of the child involved. The parents typically used the experience to make the point that "this is the way of the world" and that the children were likely to encounter even worse situations as they grew older and moved out on their own.

We believe that one of the important measures of the parents' unselfish love and concern about their adopted children may be found in their responses to the question about the birth parents. Approximately 40 percent of the parents told us that their children expressed interest in learning about their birth parents. Of those, 7 percent also wanted to locate and meet one or both of their birth parents. An additional 10 percent of the parents had provided their adopted children with whatever information they had, even prior to, or in the absence of, the children's request. Only 3 percent, out of the 40 percent of the parents whose children have asked about their birth parents, were sufficiently threatened by the child's interest to refuse to provide the information that they had.

On the question of "principle," 84 percent told us that they believe adoptees should have all the information available on their birth records when they are adults. The types of information that some of the parents would withhold included facts such as that the child was born out of wedlock, one or both parents were in prison, or the mother was a prostitute. Three percent of the parents believed that adoption records should remain closed. An additional 8 percent would place some conditions on opening such records, such as medical needs. But as we have shown earlier, the large majority of the parents believe that their adopted child should have access to as much information about the birth parents as they can provide, and they do not feel that it is a sign of disloyalty or lack of commitment to them if the child wants that informtion.

Looking at the issue from the adoptees' perspective, we found that 63 percent of the TRAs had already tried, plan to try, or think they might be interested in locating their birth parents. The others said that they do not plan to attempt to find them. The most typical response was: "I am happy with my family. My other parents gave me up." Most of the adoptees did not have deeply rooted feelings about their reasons for wanting to locate their birth parents; curiosity seemed to characterize most of their feelings. Many said, "I would like to see what I will look like when I'm older." Those for whom the issue was more traumatic were children who were adopted when they were three or more years of age, had some memory of a mother, and felt a sense of abandonment or betrayal. They expressed their feelings in the rather muted phrase: "I'll feel incomplete until I do."

At the conclusion of both of our earlier books, we emphasized that it was still too soon to draw any conclusions on two matters. One concerned the parents' evaluations of how "good," how "meaningful," how "positive" an experience their decision to adopt transracially had been; and the other pertained to our evaluation of the families' experiences; that is, whether they had lived together in a positive, loving, committed relationship. The bases for our eventual conclusions on the latter issue would be a study of the families themselves over the 12-year period, including the parents' as well as the children's responses, and our observations of the family's interactions.

We would also take into account our comparison of these families with other studies of families who have adopted transracially, as well as with our knowledge of middle class families in the urban United States. For example, in the concluding chapter of their book, McRoy and Zurcher wrote:

> The transracial and inracial adoptees in the authors' study were physically healthy and exhibited typical adolescent relationships with their parents, siblings, teachers, and peers. Similarly, regardless of the race of their adop-

tive parents, they reflected positive feelings of self-regard. Throughout the book, the authors have shown that the quality of parenting is more important than whether the black child has been inracially or transracially adopted. Most certainly, transracial adoptive parents experience some challenges different from inracial adoptive parents, but in this study, all of the parents successfully met the challenges.[3]

Gill and Jackson, in summarizing the results of their study, wrote:

We found no general evidence of the children being isolated within their families. Close and intimate family relations had developed for the large majority of the children. The children saw themselves as "belonging to this family."
 . . . in spite of their often having very little contact with other children of the same racial background, we found that the large majority of children were able to relate effectively to peers and adults outside the family. Also, there is no evidence of the children doing worse academically than their age-mates; if anything, the study children seemed to be doing better.[4]

We turn finally to the judgments made by the parents in our study about their experiences. We think the best indicator is the parents' responses to this item:

Would you advise a family like your own to adopt a nonwhite child?

We reported in the first study, when the children were between three and eight years old, that all but 3 percent of the parents said that they would urge the family to adopt (7 percent answered that as a matter of principle they would not advise anyone on such a personal, complicated issue). In the present study, conducted when the transracial adoptees were adolescents and young adults, 6 percent said that they would advise against such a decision, 1 percent were uncertain about the advice that they would give, and 8 percent would not offer advice as a matter of principle. Eighty-five percent would urge the family to adopt transracially.

Is 85 a high percentage? Compared to what—to families who have adopted inracially; to families who have only had birth children? Would more than 85 percent advise other couples to bear children? Would there not be some small percentage who would believe as a matter of principle that they should not advise people on such a personal issue; and would there not be a small category, of say 7 percent, who would feel, for many different reasons, that having children had been a mistake for them and who would be willing to generalize their experiences to others? In the end, whether 85 percent is a large or small proportion of families, whether it is an indicator that families believe transracial adoption was a success or failure, is up to the reader to decide.

We urge the reader to take note of the direct responses by the parents to the questions posed to them. They emphasized love and the desire for a child as the major reasons why anyone should want to adopt transracially. One family said, "It is the best thing that has happened to us." They warned that the families should be prepared for complications and problems—but is any child rearing free of anxiety and difficulties? Just as in 1972, the parents warned: Do not adopt for political motives; do not do it as part of a crusade, or to wave a banner, or out of white liberal guilt. They also cautioned prospective adoptive parents that the race issue could prove more complicated than they anticipated, and urged learning as much as possible about the child's racial heritage. The major and strongest messages were: "Be sure you are committed to adoption." "Adopt if you love and want children." "Pray about it, keep your motives straight; adopt because you need and love a child."

In essence, these were the messages the parents sent in 1972, in 1979, and again in 1984, when, for many of them, their TRAs had graduated from childhood into young adulthood.

NOTES

1. Rita J. Simon and Howard Altstein, *Transracial Adoption* (New York: Wiley Interscience, 1977), pp. 147–48.

2. Owen Gill and Barbara Jackson, *Adoption and Race* (New York: St. Martin's Press, 1983), p. 39.

3. Ruth G. McRoy and Louis A. Zurcher, *Transracial and Inracial Adoption* (Springfield, Ill.: Charles C. Thomas, 1983), p. 138.

4. Gill and Jackson, op. cit., p. 130.

Part III

9

Effects of Abortion, Birth Rate, and Lifestyle on Inracial and Transracial Adoptions

For the last decade or so, three persistent factors have affected adoption rates in the United States: abortions, birth rates, and lifestyle changes. Each will be discussed in the context of its influence on rates of adoption and, wherever possible, the number of transracial adoptions.

ABORTIONS

Most researchers in child welfare believe that abortion rates, particularly among unmarried females in the 15–19 age bracket, affect the number of children available for adoption. As shown by the numbers below, nonwhite women under the age of 20 were more than twice as likely to abort their pregnancies as were white women under 20.[1] By 1976, if one expands the age range to include women between the ages of 15 and 44 (i.e., child-bearing years), the rate of abortions for nonwhites exceeded that for whites by a factor of three, with the white rate actually going down slightly.[2]

Rate of Abortions per 1,000 Women Aged 20 or Less by Race, 1973

White	Nonwhite
20.6	43.8

Rate of Abortions per 1,000 Women Aged 15–44 by Race, 1976

White	Nonwhite
19.0	58.0

121

In 1977, 1.3 million abortions were recorded for all ages and races, and in 1980 the figure was 1.5 million.[3] By 1985, the rate of abortions in the United States per 1,000 live births was 426, ranging from 731 per 1,000 in New York State to 100 in Utah. The District of Columbia had an abortion rate of 1,517 per 1,000 live births.[4]

In 1982, the last year for which any data are available, the United States exceeded practically all other industrialized countries in teenage abortions.[5] As shown in the table below, U.S. rates are twice as high as those of France and Sweden, the countries with the next highest rates.

Abortion Rates per 1,000 Women, 18 Years and Younger by Country, 1982

United States	60
France	30
Sweden	30
Canada	24
England/Wales	20
Netherlands	7

Source: Nadine Brozan, "Rate of Pregnancies for U.S. Teenagers Found High in Study," New York Times, March 13, 1985, p. 1.

What conclusions can be drawn from these figures? Had abortion not been accessible to these women, particularly those less than 19 years of age, would they have seen adoption as a possible alternative and, if so, how many would have chosen it? What would the effect have been on transracial adoption? Without additional information, answers must be speculative. But it is reasonable to assume that an unknown number of black and white mothers would have surrendered their infants, thereby increasing the pool of adoptable children of both races. In doing so, TRA would in all likelihood have been affected. Given estimates of approximately 40 white couples waiting for every available white infant, white infants would have been quickly adopted, leaving free for adoption many black children.[6] Without strong efforts to place these children inracially, on a practical level transracial adoption would have been seen as a plan of choice.

BIRTH RATES

Few would argue against a general linkage between birth rates, particularly among females less than 19 years old, and the number of children available for adoption. But before any confident association can be established, other factors have to be taken into account. For example, there are questions of whether these births were to married or unmarried women, and the number of babies released for adoption. With respect to transracial adoption, it is also important to know the mother's racial background. This section examines some birth rate trends in light of adoption, and specifically TRA.

By 1982, in comparison to other Western countries, the United States was experiencing an increase in both abortion and birth rates. As shown in the chart below, the pregnancy rate for American females 15 to 19 years old was slightly more than twice those of England/Wales, Canada, and France, respectively.[7]

Birth Rates per 1,000 Women Ages 15–19 by Country, 1982

United States	96
England/Wales	45
Canada	44
France	43
Sweden	35
Netherlands	14

Source: Nadine Brozan, "Rate of Pregnancies for U.S. Teenagers Found High in Study," *New York Times*, March 13, 1985, p. 1.

What is particularly important for this discussion is the birth rate differential by race.

Birth Rate per 1,000 U.S. Women Ages 15–19 by Race, 1982

White	Black
83	163

Source: Nadine Brozan, "Rate of Pregnancies for U.S. Teenagers Found High in Study," *New York Times*, March 13, 1985, p. 1.

Black females between the ages of 15 and 19, as shown above, have a birth rate almost twice that for whites. Nationally, 55 percent of all black infants are born to unwed mothers. In some predominantly black areas, that figure is considerably higher. For example, in New York City's Harlem, 79.9 percent of all children were born to unwed mothers in 1983.[8] If there is an association between birth rate and adoption, particularly when a majority of births are to unmarried women between the ages of 15 and 19, one can assume a trend toward an increasing rate of adoption. With respect to transracial adoption and without accounting for the influence of other conditions, the fact that teenage black females are having twice the number of children as their white counterparts would, on the surface, lead one to believe that this type of child placement should be increasing.

Important as the above figures are, what must be determined is the number of children released for adoption. Some of these data are available. The National Center for Health Statistics, relying on previously published material as well as its own projections, reported that in 1971, 7.6 percent of all babies born to unwed mothers between the ages of 15 and 19 were placed for adoption. By 1982, this figure dropped to 4.6 percent. An examination of these figures by race of mother reveals that in 1971, 18.4 percent of the children born to whites were placed for adoption as compared to only 2 percent for blacks. By 1982, both races had substantially reduced the percentage of children given to adoption, with the greatest impact (not percentage reduction) on black children—7.4 percent of the white children were placed for adoption as compared to only 0.7 percent of the black children. By 1982, 6.2 percent of all births to women aged 15–19 were placed for adoption. But only 0.4 percent of black mothers made such arrangements, contrasted to 12.2 percent of white mothers.

What is striking about these figures, race notwithstanding, is the extent to which unmarried mothers of all ages (15–44) do not see adoption as an initial plan of choice. This is particularly true for black females, and therefore an important issue for transracial adoption. The fact that adoptable black infants (as opposed to children) are no longer available in any significant numbers may make the future of this type of child placement moot. The diminishing number of black children may also help explain the rise in the number of intercountry adoptions, since the rate at which white mothers are placing their children for adoption is also extremely low.

LIFESTYLE

This section highlights contraceptive use and other lifestyle changes which have affected the number of children available for adoption. First, communities and individual families no longer view unwed motherhood as negatively as they once did.[9]

Another important attribute affecting the number of adoptable children is a radical redefinition of human relationships, sexual and nonsexual. Historically, an "out-of-wedlock" woman and her "illegitimate" child were labeled as such, treated indifferently at best and as societal outcasts at worst. Since this hostility is no longer the prevailing reaction, most unwed mothers do not feel as pressured as they once did to relinquish their children. Consequently, the number of "desirable" children available for adoption has been affected. The term "desirable" is explained in the following discussion.

We noted earlier that teenage U.S. females have twice the number of children per 1,000 as their closest counterparts in England and Wales. This is not because U.S. females begin sexual activity at an earlier age, have fewer abortions, are overly represented by poor blacks, or are products of liberal social welfare policies supporting unwed motherhood. Rather, the high teenage birth rate in the United States can be explained by the comparative use of contraceptives. Not only do we have the lowest level of contraceptive use, but when using contraceptives, U.S. teenagers generally fail to use the most effective device, birth control pills.[10] One study indicated that, excluding approximately 25 percent of a teenage sample who intended to become pregnant, less than 20 percent of the remainder used contraceptives.[11]

Implications drawn from these factors for adoption must at this point be guarded. Although an overwhelming majority of teenage mothers initially choose to keep their children (with a recent study reporting a rate of 96 percent)[12] as they enter their late teens and early twenties, there is an increasing chance that they will reconsider their original rejection of the adoption alternative. But at the ages of three, four, or older, their children are much more difficult to place in adoptive homes. Then, the usual option becomes foster care with its by now well-known pitfall of permanent "temporary" placements.

It is within the context of deciding on the adoption route when a child is three years old or older that the term "desirable" is so important. Most people who want to adopt prefer an infant to any other age group. Usually, the older the child, the more difficult placement in an adoptive home becomes. In fact, although there is variation from state to state, a child's age is usually an important criterion for the "hard-to-place" category. Again, in the absence of any national figures, we have no accurate sense of how many "older" children are free for adoption, but there are some survey data available. The National Adoption Exchange indicates that 87 percent of the black children registered for adoption are between 6 and 17 years of age. The figure is 91 percent for white children.[13]

Other social and psychological influences appear to affect an unwed mother's adoption plans. Generally, there seems to be a relationship among socioeconomic status, parental influence, intact family, involvement of the infant's father, level of maturity, and the mother's willingness to place her child for adoption.

The consequences of lifestyle changes on transracial adoption are somewhat indirect but nonetheless telling. In addition to the above mentioned factors regarding individual psychosocial factors on unwed black women's adoption plans, recent data establish that these women overwhelmingly choose not to consider "offical" (e.g., court approved) adoption under practically any conditions. This should not be understood to indicate that black children are adopted less frequently than whites. What occurs is that many black infants are "informally adopted" by caring relatives and friends. No legal proceedings are involved. The practice of informal adoption is a long established historic tradition in the black community, dating from both African tribal norms and conditions of slavery in the United States.

An additional factor mitigating against court approved adoption is the generally held suspicion among a large segment of the black community toward most social agencies. Yet a fourth explanation for informal adoption is the widespread feeling in the black community that child welfare agencies have an extremely large number of adoptable black children and few potential black adoptive parents, reducing the likelihood of inracial placement. Whatever the reasons for rejecting official adoption, the result is fewer adoptable black children reaching the child welfare system. To the extent that this occurs, the opportunities for transracial adoption are reduced.

NOTES

1. Melvin Zelnik and John Kanter, "First Pregnancies to Women Aged 15-19: 1976-1977," *Family Planning Perspective* 10 (January-February 1978):11.

2. Jacqueline Darroch Forrest, Christopher Tietze, and Ellen Sullivan, "Abortion in the United States, 1976-1977," *Family Planning Perspective* 10 (September-October 1978):271.

3. "1.55 Million Abortions Reported in 1980," *New York Times*, February 23, 1982, p. A14.

4. "New York Is First in Abortion Rate," *New York Times*, March 3, 1985, p. 18.

5. Nadine Brozan, "Rate of Pregnancies for U.S. Teenagers Found High in Study," *New York Times*, March 13, 1985, p. 1.

6. Eileen Keendoya, "Adoption: New Frustration, New Hope," *Newsweek*, February 13, 1984, p. 80.

7. Brozan, op. cit., p. 1.

8. Joseph Berger, "Unwed Mothers Accounting for Third of New York Births," *New York Times*, August 13, 1984, p. 1.

9. Cynthia Leynes, "Keep or Adopt: A Study of Factors Influencing Pregnant Adolescents' Plans for Their Babies," *Child Psychiatry and Human Development* 11 (Winter 1980): 105-12; Trudy Bradley Festinger, "Unwed Mothers and Their Decisions to Keep or Surrender Children," *Child Welfare* 50 (May 1971):253.

10. "America's Pregnant Children" (editorial), *New York Times*, March 15, 1985, p. 26.

11. George Shah et al., "Unprotected Intercourse Among Unwed Teenagers," *Family Planning Perspectives* 7 (January-February 1975):36–42.

12. "Teenage Pregnancy: The Problem That Hasn't Gone Away," The Alan Guttmacher Institute, 1981, p. 27.

13. "Profile: National Adoption Exchange's Registered Children," *FACE Facts* (November 1984), p. 7.

10

Single Parent Adoption: A Continuing Alternative

In our first volume, we suggested that the benefits of inracial single parent adoption (SPA) had not been sufficiently examined as a possible alternative to transracial adoption. In fact, this practice, which was ignored by child welfare institutions until the 1960s, may hold considerable promise as an alternative for countless children currently available for adoption in foster care or group homes. Today, more than a decade after our first work, we continue to view this type of permanent child placement as a viable alternative. Our position is consistent with society's changing views of relationships, making the single parent family a more normative child-rearing environment. The women's movement in particular has had a major role in the growing prevalence and general acceptance of this type of family setting.

SINGLE PARENTHOOD

The concept of single parenthood no longer carries its historic stigma, regardless of the single parent's gender. This is indicated in the percent of single parent families who adopt and in the policies and practices created to serve this ever-increasing population. As the figures below demonstrate, the percent of such families with at least one child less than 18 years old increased 100 percent between 1970 and 1984.[1]

Percent of Single Parent Families with Children Less than 18 Years Old, of All U.S. Families

1970	1980	1984
12.9	21.5	25.7

Additionally, one study projects that "of children born in 1980, 59 percent...can expect to spend at least one year before their 18th birthday living in a single parent situation...[and] by 1990, 26.5 percent of all race children will be living with one parent only."[2] Clearly, there is convincing evidence to support the notion that single parenthood is an institutionalized form of child rearing.

SINGLE PARENT ADOPTIONS (SPAs)

Historically, SPAs were considered by adoption agencies as placements of last resort, when an adoptable child's only options were institutionalization or foster care. Even then, the only children whom agencies would make available were the most difficult to place, the "special needs" child. Race has always been a qualifying factor for this category. It is a testimonial to the paradox of child welfare practice that potential single parent adopters, defined as placements of last resort, were allowed to adopt only the children most difficult to place.

In attempting to establish valid national SPA figures, once again we operate in somewhat of a vacuum. There are no currently available, centrally located adoption figures. However, as mentioned previously, there are isolated studies, reports, articles, and so on, that suggest some figures. For example, in 1984, it was estimated that about "5 to 25 percent of all adoption placements are now being made to single people."[3] If the generally accepted estimate of 65,000 adoptions per year is used, the approximate number of SPAs last year ranged from 3,258 to 16,250. This compares to a reported total of 1.2 million adopted persons in the United States as of 1981.[4] No data are available concerning the racial breakdown of the above mentioned SPAs.

For the most part, SPAs involve women in their thirties in such traditional female occupations as teaching, social work, and nursing. But it is worth noting that one out of every seven SPAs was made to a male. The approximate range of SPAs discussed above suggests that roughly 465 of every 2,320 SPAs are made to men. To some, male SPA may smack of "trendiness" reflecting our changing expectations about men and women. But an examination of the 1984 census reveals that 945,000 fathers had total responsibility for at least one child younger than age 18. This is about three times the number for 1970, and the prediction is that this figure will continue to climb.[5]

Studies indicate that on most if not all "quality of life" measures (delinquency, suicide, emotional problems, sexual identity, etc.), children adopted by single adults appear in no way adversely affected by their experience.[6] In light of the statistics discussed above, welfare agencies responsible for finding permanent placements for children should no longer view adoption applications of single individuals with suspicion and skepticism, for these are dated reactions no longer supported by the evidence.

BLACK SINGLE PARENTHOOD

By 1985, single black women accounted for more than half of all black births. It is perhaps of greater significance that due to what has been called "the feminization of poverty," an overwhelming majority of the children born to these women—an estimated 70 percent[7]—will be raised in poverty. It is therefore not surprising that black children are overrepresented both in the ranks of the homeless (the National Black Child Development Institute stated in 1983 that roughly one of every hundred black children is without a home) and in the numbers available for adoption. For reasons discussed earlier, agencies have found it difficult to locate two-parent black families willing to adopt these children.

In 1985, three out of every five black families with children were headed by a single parent, making this type of family the rule rather than the exception. Given that 89.1 percent of single parent families of all races were female-headed in 1984, it would be safe to assume that an overwhelming majority of black single parent families would also be female-headed. But being single, male, and a household head is somewhat more common among blacks than in the general population. In 1983, for example, 4.7 percent of all black households were headed by a male, and 1.9 percent of these included children under 18; 3.3 percent of all households in the United States are male-headed.[8] In fact, some of the most successful black adoption agencies are operated by single black male adoptive parents.[9] The recommendation that "singles" are (adoptive parent) targets of opportunity is not an isolated one. In 1983, the North American Center on Adoption stated:

[An] area of concern is the failure of agencies to utilize single parents fully as resources for children. Unfounded prejudices stand in the way of children finding families. We find ourselves increasingly advocating in behalf of single parents who want to adopt. . . . we attempt to make more agencies receptive to them.[10]

The Child Welfare League of America (CWLA) assumed a similar position, but with somewhat less enthusiasm. Under the title "Qualifications of Adoptive Applicants: Marital Status," the CWLA Standards for Adoption Service stated:

Families should be selected in which a husband and wife are living together. . . . In exceptional circumstances, when the opportunity for adoption for a specific child might otherwise not be available, a single parent...should be given consideration.[11]

"It works," said the director of one of New York City's largest adoption agencies. "If it is a question of whether a child should be waiting in limbo or have the permanency of an adoptive home, then the home is the best answer."[12]

There are several reasons why targeting black singles as potential adopters might be an acceptable approach to alleviating the problem of parentless black children. To begin with, a population exists. One-third of the black population (estimated at 29 million) over the age of 18 has never married— 36.5 percent of the male population, 30.8 percent of the female population.[13] Although in 1985 the rate of unemployment for blacks (15.2 percent) was more than twice that for whites (6.2 percent), 80.6 percent of black males and 81.4 percent of black females, 25–34 years old, were employed full-time.[14] Between the ages of 35 and 44, the percentage rises to 86.5 percent of males and 88.7 percent of females. Unfortunately, there are no data examining marital status by race and employment. What is unknown, therefore, is the percent of single black men and women employed full-time. Be that as it may, an overwhelming majority of the black population between the ages of 25 and 44 is employed full-time. An unknown, but probably large, percent of them are single. Surely, given the appropriate recruitment efforts, thousands of single individuals who are willing to adopt could be located. Practically all survey research indicates that blacks are motivated to adopt, not only through the historic informal system, but also "officially" through bona fide child welfare agencies that are sensitive to the black environment.

The fact that so many waiting children are predominantly older and black makes the single employed individual all the more logical as a potential adopter. For example, in 1984 New York City had 350 children available for adoption: 65 percent were black and 20 percent were Hispanic. The average age was 12.[15] For the most part the physical needs of these children are quite different from the needs of younger children, allowing the single adoptive parent an opportunity to maintain a reasonably independent lifestyle. While the single parent's life would inevitably be altered, the adoption would not have nearly the same impact had a more physically dependent younger child been introduced into his or her life. Another important factor, in addition to well-developed programs geared toward adolescent children, is the continuing financial subsidy, up to $250 per month in New York City, to the adopter of a "hard-to-place" child.

Using statistical data and policy statements, this chapter sought to demonstrate the extent to which single parenthood is now an institutionalized form of family setting involving millions of people. We also presented the most current figures supporting our, and others', contention that single parent adoption, and in this case black single parent adoption, may be a feasible solution and thus an alternative to transracial adoption for a large segment of those awaiting adoption in the United States, older black children. We believe that agencies should concentrate considerably more of their recruitment energies toward this population and toward finding black sponsors for these programs.

NOTES

1. "One Parent Families Increasing, Study Says," *New York Times*, May 18, 1985, p. 54.

2. Paul C. Glick, "Marriage, Divorce and Living Arrangements," *Journal of Family Issues* 5 (March 1984):23-24.

3. Judy Klemesrud, "Number of Single-Parent Adoptions Grows," *New York Times*, November 19, 1984, p. C13.

4. Ibid.

5. U.S. Department of Commerce, Bureau of the Census, "Household and Family Characteristics," (Washington, March 1983), Series P-20, No. 398.

6. Joan Shireman and Penny Johnson, "Single Persons as Adoptive Parents," *Social Service Review* 50 (March 1976):103-16; Alfred Kadushin, "Single Parent Adoptions: An Overview and Some Relevant Research," *Social Service Review* 44 (September 1970):263-74.

7. Eleanor Holmes Norton, "Restoring the Traditional Black Family," *New York Times Magazine*, June 2, 1985, p. 42.

8. U.S. Department of Commerce, Bureau of the Census, *Statistical Abstract of the United States, 1985*, 105th ed. Table 36 (Washington, 1985), p. 32.

9. North American Committee on Adoptable Children, *Adoptalk* (March-April 1983).

10. *Adoption Report* 8 (1983).

11. Child Welfare League of America, Standards for Adoption Service, Revised, 1978, p. 67.

12. *New York Times*, op. cit., p. 3 .

13. U.S. Department of Commerce, Bureau of the Census, *Statistical Abstract,* Table 46, p. 37.

14. Carl T. Rowan, "Black Americans," *Baltimore Sun,* June 21, 1985, p. 15A.

15. *New York Times,* op. cit., p. C13.

11

Intercountry Adoption

Why were 8,327 foreign born nonwhite children adopted by white American families in 1984 when approximately 50,000–100,000 U.S. children in foster care were legally free for adoption (U.S. Department of Justice, Immigration and Naturalization Service)? Why were almost 85 percent of the children who were placed by one of New York City's largest adoption agencies foreign born?[1] Why is it more difficult for white families to adopt parentless nonwhite children within U.S. borders than children born in Pusan, Korea, or Bogota, Columbia?

Many of these questions can be answered by examining the social characteristics of America's waiting children and the adoption practices of the agencies responsible for them. In the United States, most children available for adoption in 1985 were older, nonwhite, physically and/or emotionally handicapped, or part of a sibling group. To a large extent, intercountry adoption (ICA) can be explained by the fact that so many of these children are nonwhite, predominantly black. It appears that many agencies continue to frown upon and therefore discourage adoption across racial lines. In contrast, the procedures involved for an ICA are comparatively simple, and the results in many cases are remarkably quick. These developments clearly operate in favor of ICA.

BRIEF HISTORY OF ICA

Intercountry adoption is the (unintended) result of efforts by the United States and other Western countries to rescue orphaned children after World War II.[2] Religious institutions were largely instrumental in locating permanent homes for these children with adoptive parents in Western countries. The Korean War, following shortly after World War II, resulted in the addition of thousands of abandoned and orphaned Korean children to the ranks of the homeless. Again, the United States and its Western allies attempted to locate permanent homes for as many of these children as possible through adoptions by their own nationals.

Concurrently, for reasons explained earlier, Western societies began to experience a shortage of natively available adoptable children, while the demand for adoption remained high. Couples seeking to adopt went beyond Korea in their search for children, to other parts of Asia, Latin America, and India. Regardless of location, all these countries had three features in common: they were developing, Third World, and nonwhite. Children adopted from these countries would therefore be both transracially and transculturally transplanted. Some people voiced a concern that these children would soon experience not only the racial confusion forecast for TRAs but cultural estrangement as well.

Not all attempts by Westerners to adopt children from other countries were successful. When thousands of children were left orphaned and/or abandoned as a result of the Nigerian civil war in the 1960s, Nigeria refused adoption offers from several Western countries.[3] Guatemala jailed several U.S. citizens involved in intercountry adoption activities.[4] Brazil suddenly and without explanation ended ICA, barring at the airport more than a dozen adoptive mothers and their children from leaving the country.[5] South Vietnam virtually eliminated ICA as a result of the "baby lift fiasco in 1975."[6]

ICA FIGURES AND SOME PROBLEMS

In 1985, a variation of the following is a common ad in most U.S. newspapers:

> *Adoption* Young professional couple, religious, happily married, unable to have children. Desire to adopt white newborn. Will have loving home and all the advantages in life. All medical, legal and birth related expenses paid. Confidential.[7]

Such a desire to adopt is representative of a continuing if not increasing national trend, dramatized by the following numbers. In 1975, the Los Angeles County Adoption Agency, one of the largest adoption agencies in the United States, reported that it placed one-tenth the number of children it did in 1965.[8] It was reported that in 1983 approximately 2 million U.S. families attempted to adopt parentless children. Less than 3 percent were able to do so.[9] In 1970, 80 percent of the infants born to unwed U.S. mothers were surrendered for adoption. In 1984, the trend was reversed; 80 percent of all children born to unwed females were kept by them.[10] Thus, the U.S. demand for

healthy adoptable infants has, if anything, increased, and the available supply of legally free for adoption children has decreased. Market forces have
directed potential adoptive parents to other sources. The following figures reflect the extent to which Americans have turned to ''other sources,'' namely,
intercountry adoption.

Number of Intercountry Adoptions by Year*

1948-1962	—	19,230
1963-1975	—	34,475
1976	—	6,552
1977	—	6,493
1978	—	5,309
1979	—	4,864
1980	—	5,139
1981	—	4,868
1982	—	5,749
1983	—	7,127
1984	—	8,327

*End of fiscal year (Immigration and Naturalization Service, Statistical Anal-
ysis Branch, ''Immigrant Orphans Admitted to the United States by Country or Region of Birth.'')

Between 1948 and 1975, Americans adopted 108,133 children born in other
countries; approximately half (54,428) were adopted between 1976 and 1984.
It is noteworthy that more than 70 percent of all ICAs were born in four countries: Korea, Colombia, India, and Mexico, and among those four countries
more than half came from Korea. The remaining ICAs were born in other
nonwhite developing countries such as El Salvador, the Philippines, Honduras,
Sri Lanka, and Guatemala.

There are two highly important characteristics of these children which
stand out: age at adoption and race. Practically all the adopted children were
less than two years old. The four countries from which 70 percent of all ICAs
were born are ''nonwhite'' and, in varying degrees, ''developing nations.''
The fact that ICAs are almost exclusively from nonwhite countries supports
the position that we took at the conclusion of our second work: although the
TRA of native born children has largely been eliminated, the next ''genera-
tion'' of TRAs would be foreign born children brought to this country for
adoption.

When demand exceeds supply, the potential exists for finding alternative
means of obtaining the scarce item. This has been the case with adoption. Although the number of ICAs in the United States continues to increase, there
are more couples who want to adopt than there are legally available children.

The U.S. State Department has identified two problem areas in this regard: (1) attempts to obtain illegal documents for a foreign born child, and (2) illegal practices by individuals who promise rapid delivery of foreign born adoptable children.[11]

The first problem exists when potential adoptive parents fraudulently attempt to obtain either U.S. visas or passports for their yet-to-be-adopted child. The second dilemma occurs when couples, eager to adopt, pay large amounts of money in the United States or abroad to individuals who claim that they will deliver a healthy, legally free for adoption infant and/or "speed up" the adoption process.

Additionally, many couples do not realize that U.S. citizenship is not automatic upon legal adoption. Foreign born children remain nationals of their country of origin until they apply for and are granted citizenship. It is also highly recommended that any ICA be finalized in an American court, even though the child may have been legally adopted abroad. If the above procedures are followed, most forseeable difficulties in ICA can be avoided.

ICA FROM KOREA

In our second study we presented a brief history of ICA from Korea through the late 1970s.[12] This section will discuss some important developments which have occurred since that time.

Clearly, the most significant post-1980 development is that Korea remains the single most important source for Westerners, particularly U.S. citizens, seeking to adopt othe nations' children. Fifty-five percent of all foreign born children adopted by U.S. citizens between 1976 and 1981 came from Korea.[13] In 1983 and 1984, that figure rose to 62 percent and 69 percent, respectively.[14]

This high proportion of Korean ICAs has its roots primarily in Korea's history. Korea basically developed into a nation without any real ethnic minorities. For over a hundred years Korea was so isolated that it was known as the "Hermit Kingdom." Mixed blood children and those classified as illegitimate were and continue to be culturally unacceptable. In fact, Confucian teaching disapproves of sexual promiscuity, and Korean law reflects an inherent discrimination against children born to unmarried women. There is, for example, no statute mandating any type of governmental assistance to children born out of wedlock.[15] Koreans rarely accept, let alone adopt, those defined as social outcasts (e.g., the "illegitimate").

If the majority of ICAs from Korea were mixed race children, the above discussion might help to explain Korea's policy. It is our impression, however, that a large percentage of children adopted from Korea are products of two Korean parents. How, then, can one explain Korea's attitude toward large-scale ICA of "pure" Korean infants? The answer stems from contemporary Korean demographics and social policies resulting from them. In a country where, in 1981, 20 percent of the population accounted for about 50 percent of the national income, it is not surprising that only 2.9 percent of Korea's annual budget was allocated to the Ministry of Health and Social Affairs, of which 32.5 percent was designated for child welfare. The latter figure represented 0.06 percent of Korea's total budget in 1981.[16] Clearly, the amount of money earmarked for child welfare, under which adoption services fall, is grossly insufficient. Moreover, prior to 1981 the government supported only institutionalized orphans. Children of the poor who remained at home and children born to unmarried women received no government support. In fact, of the nearly 56,000 single parent families eligible for assistance, only 716 received any form of aid.[17]

In this situation, where most mothers of mixed race and/or "illegitimate" children have no means of family or financial support, abandonment of their babies becomes a solution. The results of this "solution" account to a large degree for the numbers of available children from Korea. These children are a "surplus" population, a cohort for whom, because of the past, there is no present or future.

Recently, Korea announced a program not only to reduce but eventually to eliminate intercountry adoption. It hopes to achieve this by increasing domestic adoption and decreasing ICA by 10 percent each year.[18] In an attempt to begin curbing ICA, Korea announced the following regulations, which are important as a signal of the government's increasing sensitivity to large numbers of children leaving the country as well as because of the restrictions they impose.

> Parents should be no younger than 25 or older than 45.
> A couple must be married for at least 3 years.
> No more than 4 children in a family.
> An age range of no more than 15 years between husband and wife.
> No more than 40 years difference between parents and child and no
>   less than 20 years age difference.
> Child adopted should be youngest in family.
> One year minimum between adoptions.
> Suggested period of 6 months for one parent to remain at home with
>   newly adopted child.
> Suggested that childless couples should initially adopt an infant.
> Sibling groups no longer will be separated.
> No simultaneous non-related adoptions.[19]

The reduction and ultimate elimination of ICA from Korea is acknowledged to be an extremely ambitious goal, a statement of ultimate intent more than a set objective. Given the ambivalence of views on intercountry adoptions, it is not surprising that shortly after the government announced its new regulations, an article appeared in the English-language *Korean Times* which stated: "The Health-Social Affairs Ministry will push ahead intensively...the adoption of orphans by foreign families...[and] ease restrictions on the selection of countries."[20] In our opinion it appears that as long as large numbers of "hard-to-place" children are abandoned, requiring costly programs for their care, the Korean government will reluctantly continue to look upon ICA in a favorable light.

THE SWEDISH EXPERIENCE

Intercountry adoption is not only a U.S. phenomenon. Western Europe has been experiencing ICA at least since the mid-1960s from the same countries that allow their children to be adopted by U.S. citizens. While on a trip to Korea, one of us was told that for every child sent to the United States for adoption purposes, four are sent to Western Europe.

Sweden is of particular interest. In 1982, in a country with a fraction of the U.S. population (about 8 million), there are in excess of 20,000 ICAs.[21] As the figures below demonstrate, from 1977 to 1980, approximately 1,500 foreign born children arrived every year in Sweden for adoption purposes. By the 1980s, the figure rose to between 1,500 and 2,000 each year.[22]

Swedish ICA, Year and Region*

	Asia		Latin America		Other	
	Number	Percent	Number	Percent	Number	Percent
1977	1350	72.3	432	23.2	84	4.5
1978	1072	65.6	469	28.7	93	5.7
1979	823	59.4	509	36.8	53	3.8
1980	1085	63.7	547	32.1	71	4.2

*"ICA: A View from Latin America," Francisco J. Pilotti, *Child Welfare* 64 (January-February 1985):25.

It is estimated that 1 out of every 50 "new" children in Sweden is an intercountry adoptee who possesses almost the same characteristics as intercountry adoptees coming into the United States. For example, by the mid-1980s, about 80 percent of the children were adopted when they were less than three years old and were born either in the Orient or Latin America (approximately 50-50). Of the Oriental children, two-thirds were born in Korea.[23]

The fact that a large percentage of American couples seeking to adopt prefer babies or children under three years of age, who are in extremely short supply in the United States but more available in other nations, largely accounts for the ever-increasing numbers of intercountry adoptees. Our guess is that, unless other countries implement policies that reduce (or perhaps even eliminate) available numbers of children for adoption, American families who want to adopt will continue to look to the children of other countries as a solution to short supply here. Since these children represent a different type of transracial adoption (e.g., transcultural), it remains to be seen whether their long-term experiences will be similar to those of native born nonwhites, transracially adopted. As of 1985, data describing intercountry adoptees' overall adjustment match information about transracial adoptees. The large majority appear to be enjoying positive experiences.[24]

One family characterized their experiences in this manner:

In this claim we are not saying that bicultural adoptive families are qualitatively unique—*all* children are vulnerable to insecurity and isolation; *all* parents are plagued by uncertainty and guilt—we are just suggesting that the normal problems of family life become magnified in a bicultural adoptive setting. The problems have the same shape, they are just larger. But there remains a very distinct possibility that the joys of parenting are also larger in an adoptive family. To create life where there was none offers its own rewards, but these are exceeded by the joys of creating hope where there was despair.[25]

NOTES

1. Maryann Bucknum, "The Baby Business," *McCall's*, June 1985, p. 88.
2. Barbara Joe, "In Defense of Intercountry Adoption," *Social Service Review* 52, no 1 (March 1978), p. 1, is one of the best articles on the historical perspective of ICA.
3. Alfred Kadushin, *Child Welfare Services* (New York: Macmillan, 1980), p. 506.
4. Genevieve De Hoyos et al., "Adoption Differentials in Three Cultural Settings." Paper presented at the First International Conference on Pediatric Social Work, Chicago, August 14, 1982.
5. Warren Hoge, "Brazil Blocks 13 Adoptions by Americans," *New York Times*, October 11, 1981.
6. Kadushin, op. cit., p. 506.
7. Personal ad. *Baltimore Sun*, June 30, 1985, p. E2.
8. U.S. Senate, Committee on the Judiciary, Subcommittee on Courts, March 16, 1984, p. 26.
9. Ibid., p. 23.
10. Ibid., p. 26.
11. Ibid., p. 47.
12. Rita J. Simon and Howard Altstein, *Transracial Adoption: A Follow-up* (Lexington, Mass.: Lexington Books, 1981), p. 97.
13. Immigration and Naturalization Service, Statistical Analysis Branch, *Statistical Year Books, 1980, 1981, 1982, 1983, 1984.* (Washington D.C. Goverment Printing Office).
14. Ibid., 1982.

15. Chin Kim and Timothy Carroll, "Intercountry Adoption of South Korean Orphans: A Lawyer's Guide," *Journal of Family Life* 14 (1975):223–53.

16. Houn Taek Tahk, "Social Welfare and Adoption in Korea." Paper presented at International Seminar on Adoption, Frankfurt, Germany, May 17-19, 1982.

17. Ibid.

18. Ibid.

19. "New Regulations From Korea," *FACE Facts* 8, no. 3 (March 1984):7.

20. "O'seas Emigration Pushed," *Korea Times*, October 16, 1981, p. 7.

21. *Adoption in Sweden.* (Stockholm: National Board of Intercountry Adoption, 1982).

22. Ibid., p. 4.

23. Ibid.

24. Gunilla Andersson, "Intercountry Adoption in a Swedish Perspective." Paper presented at the International Congress on Adoption, Eilat, Israel, May 9–14, 1982; Christopher Bagley and Loretta Young, "The Long Term Adjustment and Identity of a Sample of Intercountry Adopted Children," *International Social Work* 23 (1980):16–22; Dong S. Kim, "Issues in Transracial and Transcultural Adoption," *Social Casework* 59 (1980):477–86; Burton Sokoloff, Jean Carlo, and Hien Pham, "A Five Year Follow-up of Vietnamese Refugee Children," *Clinical Pediatrics* 23 (October 1984):565.

25. Marilyn and Loyal Rue, "Reflections on Bicultural Adoptions," in *Adoption* edited by Philip Bean (London: Tavistock 1984):253.

Concluding Remarks and Recommendations

Twelve years have gone by since our initial contact with the families described in this volume. We met them in 1972, when they had only recently embarked on a largely untravelled and potentially difficult road of adopting children of different racial backgrounds than their own, some of whom had mental and physical disabilities, while at the same time parenting children to whom they had given birth. As ready as they might have been for hostility and rejection by their relatives, friends, and neighbors, they were least prepared for the attacks upon them by blacks, native American leaders, and professional social work groups, who charged them with everything from ignorance to participation in racial genocide. The results of the second and third surveys showed that, with a few exceptions, all of the parents believed that they had done well by the children whom they adopted and that, had they not adopted them, the children would have spent their childhood in an institution or in one or more foster homes. The parents repeatedly emphasized that they made their decision to adopt because they wanted a child and were prepared to love and care for it regardless of the child's racial or personal background. Again, with few exceptions, all of the parents are still committed to that view and are willing to urge other families to adopt transracially.

As we said many times, the children seem even more committed to their adoptive parents than the other way around. For the children, even during these sensitive, complicated years of adolescence, their adoptive parents are the only family they have and the only set of parents they want. Some of the family relationships have been rocky, accusative, and angry—and some remain so—yet they are a family and they are fully committed to one another.

At the end of both the 1972 and 1979 studies, we emphasized the tentativeness of our conclusions. While focusing on the positive experiences that we were able to report, we also stressed how young the children were and how many difficult periods lay ahead. This time, we believe that the families have reached a different stage. In many of them, some children are married and living on their own; in others, some are away at school. Practically all of the children, even the youngest, are adolescents. The quality of the relationships is established, and the ties are not likely to be severed by some future event. The families have weathered the most difficult years of child rearing, and the large majority have come through the experience committed to each other and intact.

It would be foolish to say that these families will have smooth sailing from here on. Who can say that with authority or certainty about any set of family relationships? But we can and do emphasize that more than 12 years have elapsed; and the large majority are still convinced of the rightness of their decision to adopt, still optimistic about their relationships with each other.

PRACTICAL IMPLICATIONS

There are some social workers who perceive both themselves and their profession as having little power to change or influence important events in people's lives or in society's behavior. We believe that it is important, therefore, to point out that there are many situations involving critical life decisions in which social workers are enormously influential. Social workers often recommend who should be admitted into a nursing facility, hospice, or home for the aged, or they determine whether to recommend children's removal from their parents—these are clearly decisions of great significance to the persons involved. The acceptance or rejection of a family's application to adopt a child is another striking example of social workers' authority. Since the social work profession almost completely dominates the field of child welfare, the "rise and fall" of transracial adoption is also a direct result of social work practice.

An examination of available figures from a variety of sources shows conclusively that transracial adoption no longer occurs in any appreciable numbers. As we stated at the conclusion of our second study, TRA was not halted because data indicated that it was a failure, that adoptees and/or their adoptive families suffered any damaging social or psychological effects. It was not stopped because transracial adoptees were experiencing racial confusion or negative self-images. It did not end because there were no longer any non-white children in foster care or in institutions requiring permanent placements. It was not eradicated because the supply of families willing and able to adopt a child of another race was exhausted. Transracial adoption died because child welfare agencies no longer saw it as politically expedient, even though none of the 50 states recognizes race as a sufficient factor in denying an adoption.

RECOMMENDATIONS

What practical recommendations are suggested by the data in this work to agencies charged with locating permanent placements for nonwhite children? Clearly, agency efforts should be initially directed at locating permanent inracial placements for their children. There are data that support the efficacy of recruiting inracial adoptive placements. But, successful as these programs have been, they have not significantly reduced the great numbers of nonwhite children requiring permanent placements.

We believe that there should be exploration of all permanent and viable inracial opportunities. But where no suitable placement is located, applications from white families seeking to adopt transracially should be examined in as objective and unbiased a manner as possible. We do not believe that inracial foster care placement is preferable to transracial adoption, because by definition foster care is temporary placement. It is a testimonial to the failure of our child welfare system that in many instances it has become permanent.

Most practicing social workers recognize the adage that foster care is a good placement because it is a quiet placement. If the foster family does not complain, a social worker should not ''rock the boat.'' We recommend, however, rocking the boat by continuous reevaluation of inracial foster placements when potentially adoptive white families become available. This is not a radical suggestion. Foster care was created to serve as an interim measure, a holding pattern until a child's family of origin regained its resources or until another permanent placement was found. Even the best foster placement remains psychologically temporary in the minds of all concerned. The presence of a potentially adoptive white family could be used as a stimulant to urge the foster family to consider adoption. The use of subsidies for eligible families has resulted in many adoptions which would not have occurred if such programs were not available.

The authors of this work are not so naive as to think that objectively gathered data such as ours will reverse a trend that, in our estimation, is by and large politically motivated. One need only read the most recent statements by the National Association of Black Social Workers' president in the *Congressional Record* of June 25, 1985, to understand how vehemently opposed this organization remains to TRA.[1]

We see reason for hope in those professional social workers who have direct caseload responsibility. The message offered by our work is that transracial adoption should not be automatically excluded as one of several permanent placement options. Adoption, in almost all cases, is a ''forever'' placement, whereas the best foster care placement is by definition temporary. Where no appropriate permanent inracial placement can be found for a nonwhite child, the results of this study demonstrate that TRA should be seriously considered.

We do not deny that a social worker who recommends placing a nonwhite child with a white family may be at risk. But the risk to which we refer is not one to the child or the adoptive family. Rather, the risk may involve agency and collegial pressure not to support this type of permanent placement. The implications of our findings oppose the negation of transracial adoption as a permanent placement choice and translate into support for further investigation of this type of placement when it is deemed feasible by the social worker. The refusal to view transracial adoption as an option violates a basic tenet that the field of social work has been laboring to establish over the past several decades: to base the interventions of social workers on grounds that can be supported empirically.

NOTE

1. Excerpt from testimony by President William T. Merritt, National Association of Black Social Workers, Senate Hearings, Committee on Labor and Human Resources, "Barriers to Adoption," National Association of Black Social Workers, 271 West 125th Street, New York, NY 10027, Tuesday, June 25, 1985, 10 A.M.

TRANSRACIAL ADOPTIONS

Some experts and others believe that transracial adoption (white families adopting Black children) will alleviate the problem of the large numbers of Black children in care. However, this is a myth because:

- The majority of *white families* who would consider transracial adoption *want healthy infants and toddlers*. However, the *majority of Black children in need of adoption are eight years old and older and are special needs children.*
- The placement of Black children in white families does not decrease the large number of Black children in need of families.
- Black children who have grown up in white families suffer severe identity problems. On the one hand, the white community has not fully accepted them and, on the other hand they have had no significant contact with Black people.
- Black children adopted transracially, often do not develop coping mechanisms necessary to function in a society that is inherently racist against African Americans.
- Transracial adoptions in the long term often disrupt and the Black children are returned to the foster care program. Children suffer a further sense of rejection as they try to understand why their adoptive as well as their biological parents gave them up.
- In addition, what about the over 50 percent hard to place white children who are not being adopted?

We are opposed to transracial adoption as a solution to permanent placement for Black children. We have an ethnic, moral and professional obligation to oppose transracial adoption. We are therefore *legally* justified in our efforts to protect the rights of Black children, Black families, and the Black community. We view the placement of Black children in white homes as a hostile act against our community. It is a blatant form of race and cultural genocide.

Selected Bibliography

Anderson, David C. *Children of Special Value—Interracial Adoption in America*. New York: St. Martin's Press, 1971.

Bean, Philip, ed. *Adoption*. London: Tavistock, 1984.

Benet, Mary K. *The Politics of Adoption*. New York: The Free Press, 1976.

Billingsley, Andrew, and Jeanne Giovanonni. *Child of the Storm: Black Children and American Child Welfare*. New York: Harcourt Brace Jovanovich, 1982.

Clark, Kenneth B., and Mamie P. Clark. "Racial Identification and Preference in Negro Children." In E. Maccoby, T. Newcomb, and E. Hartley, eds. *Reading in Social Psychology*. New York: Holt, 1958.

Day, Dawn. *The Adoption of Black Children*. Lexington, Mass.: Lexington Books, 1979.

Fanshel, David. *Far from the Reservation: The Transracial Adoption of American Indian Children*. Metuchen, N.J.: Scarecrow Press, 1972.

Feigelman, William, and Arnold Silverman. *Chosen Children: New Patterns of Adoptive Relationships*. New York: Praeger, 1983.

Gill, Owen, and Barbara Jackson. *Adoption and Race*. New York: St. Martin's Press, 1983.

Goodman, Mary Ellen. *Race Awareness in Young Children*. New York: Collier, 1964.

Grow, Lucille J., and Deborah Shapiro. *Black Children, White Parents: A Study of Transracial Adoption*. New York: Child Welfare League of America, 1972.

Jaffee, Benson, and David Fanshel. *How They Fared in Adoption: A Follow-up Study*. New York: Columbia University Press, 1970.

Kadushin, Alfred. *Child Welfare Services*. New York: Macmillan, 1980.

Kirk, H. David. *Shared Fate*. New York: Free Press, 1964.

Koh, Frances M. *Oriental Children in American Homes*. Minneapolis: East-West Press, 1981.

Ladner, Joyce. *Mixed Families*. New York: Anchor Press, Doubleday, 1977.

McRoy, Ruth G., and Louis A. Zurcher. *Transracial and Inracial Adoptees*. Springfield, Ill.: Charles C. Thomas, 1983.

Morland, J. Kenneth. *Racial Attitudes in School Children: From Kindergarten Through High School*. Washington, D.C.: U.S. Department of Health, Education, and Welfare, Office of Education, National Center for Educational Research and Development, 1972.

Nutt, Thomas E., and John A. Synder. *Transracial Adoption*. Cambridge, Mass.: Massachusetts Institute of Technology, 1973.

Porter, Judith D.R. *Black Child, White Child: The Development of Racial Attitudes*. Cambridge, Mass.: Harvard University Press, 1971.

Rosenberg, Morris. *Society and the Adolescent Self-Image*. Princeton, N.J.: Princeton University Press, 1965.

Rosenberg, Morris, and Roberta G. Simmons. *Black and White Self-Esteem: The Urban School Child*. Arnold M. and Caroline Rose Monograph Series. Washington, D.C.: American Sociological Association, 1971.

Tizard, Barbara. *Adoption: A Second Chance*. London: Open Books, 1977.

Valk, Margaret. *Korean-American Children in American Adoptive Homes*. New York: Child Welfare League of America, 1957.

Verma, G. K., and C. Bagley, eds. *Race Education and Identity*. London: Macmillan, 1979.

Zastrow, Charles H. *Outcome of Black Children-White Parents Transracial Adoptions*. San Francisco: R. & E. Research Associates, 1977.

Index

About the Authors

RITA J. SIMON is the Dean of the School of Justice at The American University in Washington, D.C. In addition to authoring two earlier works on transracial adoption, she is the author of *Public Opinion and the Immigrant: Print Media Coverage 1880-1980, Women and Crime, Continuity and Change: A Study of Two Ethnic Communities in Israel*, and several books on the jury system. Dean Simon is a former editor of the *American Sociological Review* and *Justice Quarterly*.

HOWARD ALTSTEIN is a professor at the School of Social Work of the University of Maryland. He is the co-author with Rita J. Simon of two earlier books on transracial adoption, *Transracial Adoption* and *Transracial Adoption: A Follow-up*, and the author of several articles on child welfare.